The Life and Times of Texas Fosbery

The Cariboo and Beyond

To Harvey + Yvonne —
I hope you enjoy
this trip into B.C. history.
Sincerely,
Karen Piffko
Oct 26, 2000.

Karen Piffko

Heritage House

Canadian Cataloguing in Publication Data

Piffko, Karen, 1942-
    The life and times of Texas Fosbery

    Includes index.
    ISBN 1-895811-93-7

    1. Fosbery, Tex. 2. Cariboo Region (B.C.)—Biography. I. Title.
FC3845.C3Z49 2000   971.1'7504'092   C00-910118-7
F1089.C3P53 2000

First Edition 2000

    Heritage House acknowledges the financial support of Heritage
Canada through the Book Publishing Industry Development Program
and of the British Columbia Arts Council for our publishing activities.

Cover design and layout by Darlene Nickull
Edited by Terri Elderton

HERITAGE HOUSE PUBLISHING COMPANY LTD.
Unit #108-17665 66A Avenue, Surrey, BC V3S 2A7

Printed in Canada   Canadä

1

Early Life in the Chilcotin
(1926-1933)

Boom! Boom! The sound of the blasts from the double-barrelled shotgun filled the night air. The horses were bucking and bolting. The cowboys were grabbing leather. Some stayed in their saddles and some were thrown to the ground.

My dad, Percy Henry Vincent Fosbery, was slapping his thigh and laughing out loud as he watched the rodeo from the porch. He'd invited the local cowboys over to his place on Big Creek in the Cariboo for a Saturday night get-together. He knew that they'd have a few drinks under their belt before they arrived, and he decided to get the party started as they rode through the gate.

Earlier he had opened the gate, attached the shotgun to the gatepost, and run a string from the triggers. He tied the strings to the opposite gatepost and waited for the first horse to run through. The prank was a great success. No one was hurt, and as everyone laughed about it later, they were already making plans to top that one.

You might say that the Cariboo is in my blood. A series of events had brought first my dad to the Big Creek country, later my mother, and later still myself and my brother Tony.

My grandfather, Percy Vincent Fosbery, travelled to the Yukon during the gold rush of 1898. He came from England, hiked the Chilkoot Trail, built a boat, and went down the Yukon to the Klondike River. He didn't find much gold, so he headed south to the Omineca area of northwestern British Columbia where he had more success.

My grandfather made several trips to the west in the following years. He probably would have stayed in this country, but he had a wife and children in England. On one of his trips he received a letter from my grandmother that said, "You'll have to choose between that country and your family. We need you."

In 1913 my dad had just finished boarding school in Bristol when my grandmother's friend, Mrs.Church, came from British Columbia to visit. Mrs. Church said that she would pay my dad's fare to Canada if he would agree to work on their ranch for a year for $10 a month. My dad had been thinking about going to Canada and this seemed like a good opportunity. He accepted her offer and they began the journey to his new home.

When he stepped off the train at Ashcroft and met Mr.Church, he introduced himself by saying, "My name is Bob." He wanted a simpler name for his new life in Canada.

Mr.Church was driving a horse-drawn buggy called a democrat. It was a four-day trip to the ranch, and my dad walked much of the way. He wanted to get to know the country. They gave him a .22 rifle and he went ahead to shoot grouse and rabbits, which they ate on their journey.

My dad worked on the ranch with the Church family. There was Dick and Percy and several girls. They all worked at clearing the land by hand, building fences, milking cows, and doing other jobs necessary to create a ranch in the wilderness.

When World War I began in 1914, my dad decided to go back to England to join the army. He spent the rest of the war on the front lines. Although he wasn't wounded, he developed some serious respiratory problems from his years in the trenches.

He returned to the Chilcotin after the war. Through the Soldier's Settlement Company he got a loan and bought 160 acres of ranchland along Big Creek. It had a new log house on it, so he

Thank-yous to—

Ruth Severson of Big Lake for her help
and advice with the computer aspect of
producing this manuscript;

My friend Jessie for her encouragement
and for sharing her home, giving me the
freedom to work on this project;

Tex for providing one of the most
interesting life stories I've ever heard.

This book is for Tex, his family, and his
friends.

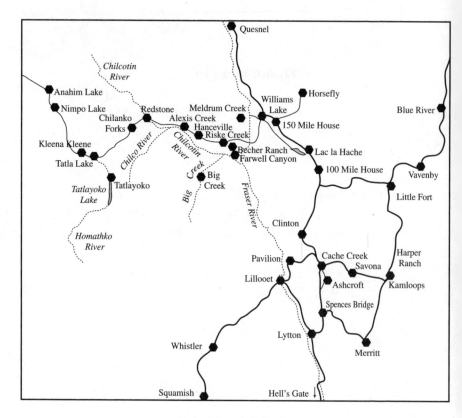

Central British Columbia

Contents

Foreword—by Veera Bonner   7

1   Early Life in the Chilcotin   9
(1926-1933)

2   Growing Up in the Okanagan   19
(1933-1942)

3   Cowboy Life for Me   28
(1942-1945)

4   Moiling for Gold—and Other Things   62
(1946-1947)

5   Something Fishy   93
(1947-1951)

6   Skinning Cats in Terrace and the Yukon   112
(1951-1954)

7   In Business With Tony   127
(1954-1955)

8   Opening Up Northwestern B.C.   138
(1955-1958)

9   Learning to Fly   148
(1958-1966)

10   More Road Building   165
(1964-1969)

11   Beginning of the End   176
(1969-1970)

Epilogue   180

Notes   185

Index   186

About the Author   192

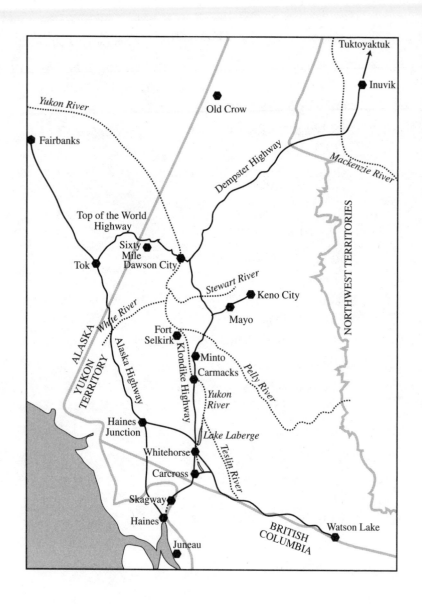

Yukon, Alaska, and Northwest Territories

Foreword

by Veera Bonner

Tex Fosbery's name is known far and wide. He's interested in everything and everybody—energetic and charming. Tex meets life head on: working, playing, travelling, and getting the most out of life. He has friends everywhere and believes in keeping in touch—one of the few in this busy world who takes time to be a friend.

He loves the Yukon and he loves flying and wisely combines the two, spending much time in the north. He is a good pilot. His yellow Cessna on floats is as familiar as the youthful figure stepping out of it.

A visit from Tex is always welcome. We look forward to walking with him through the pages of this book.

Congratulations, Tex!

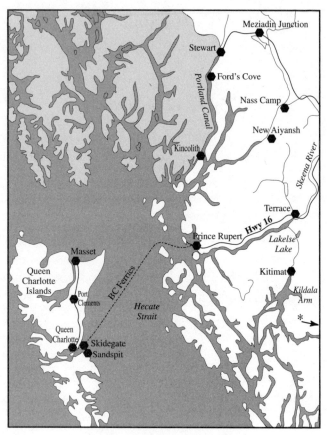

* Kemano, Tahtsa Lake and Sandifer Lake.

Northwestern British Columbia

settled in to start ranching. He put up some hay and bought a few cows which he branded with his "Bar 5."

My mother, Eve Mary Napier, born in 1904, was of Scottish, English, and Danish descent. She and her sister Esme attended boarding school in Nairobi, Kenya. Her father, Egbert Napier, was in the British army during World War I. He was killed in Belgium and buried in Flander's Field. Shortly after his death their mother remarried, and the girls were sent to a cooking school in Vancouver.

My mother read an ad in the paper for a chore-girl for a ranch at Big Creek. She applied and got the job. She took the train to Ashcroft and then rode to the 150 Mile House in an open touring car that was used as a stage. There she was met and taken out to the Blenkinsops' Bell Ranch.

My dad heard about her arrival and decided to ride over and meet her. I guess they both liked what they saw because they started going together, and in 1925 they were married.

I was born on April 27, 1926. Dr. Charters from Alexis Creek attended the birth, which took place at home. My brother Tony was born at Alexis Creek on December 23, 1927.

Life was pretty primitive, and there were many hardships for everyone in those early years. We lived about a hundred miles from Williams Lake, the nearest town. We didn't go there very often because of the distance and the poor quality of the road.

My dad owned a Star touring car at the time. My mother told me of one trip we made when I was six months old. We were going up the Chilko Ranch hill, which was dry and very sandy. The car was jumping and bouncing around as it struggled to get to the top. When it got there, my mother looked around to the back seat to see how I was doing. I wasn't there! The back door had flown open and I had slid out. They ran back down the hill and there I was lying beside the track in the sand, apparently unhurt.

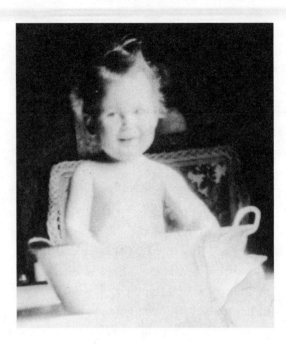

Tex, age one sitting in the bathtub on the kitchen table at Big Creek in 1928. It didn't take much water for a bath.

In 1928 my dad got rid of that car. He went up to Quesnel and bought a brand new Model A for $500. He removed the lid of the rumble seat, built a box for it, and made a pickup. That's where Tony and I rode most of the time.

We also slept there when our parents went to dances at the Big Creek Hall. We'd lie there looking up at the stars. One time my mother had given us each a nickel. We were playing with them and Tony swallowed his. He started to cry so bad that I went to find our parents. I wasn't very big, but I managed to get the door of the hall open. It was so loud in there. I was scared to death, but I went in among all those people. I finally found my mother and dad and they came out to the car. They told Tony that there was nothing they could do about it. They said that the next time he went to the bathroom he might be able to find his nickel.

Although things were tough sometimes, I'm glad that I was raised on the ranch. I've always loved the wide open spaces and

Tony enjoying the spring sunshine at
Big Creek in 1929. Notice the willow playpen.

the ranch animals, especially horses. My dad had five hay meadows where we put up the hay each summer and fed it out to the cows each winter. There was the Home Place, the Marston Place, Cooper Creek, Dolly Meadow, and Green Mountain Meadow (later known as Fosbery Meadow). We'd start at home and move from one meadow to the next. We were nomads!

My mother and dad cut the hay with horse-drawn mowers. They hired some of the Indians to actually put up the hay, using their own horses and slips and stacking poles. They were paid by the ton, so my dad would measure up the stack by throwing a long tape over it one way and then the other and cross-sectioning the volume. Two of the families who worked for my dad were the Jeffs and the Quilts.

Another fellow who contracted there was Laceese. One day he was pitching hay onto his slip. Tony and I were yapping away at him and I guess he got tired of listening to us. He stuck his pitchfork into the ground, pulled out his jackknife and said, "You come here an' I cut your nut. You come here an' I cut your nut."

Bob and Eve Fosbery (with Tex in her arms) in the horse-drawn sleigh. They had supplies in the trunk and were heading out to the meadows to feed cattle.

Well Tony and I took off on the run. I guess he was just fooling, because when we looked back across the meadow he was still laughing. We never bothered him again.

Every so often the Indians sent someone down to the Chilko Ranch Store with a packhorse to get supplies. They'd also get a big bag of sugar and some peaches to make homebrew. I remember hearing them hooting and hollering and having a great time down in their camp.

One day they didn't want to work because one of them was very sick. One fellow rode all the way to Stoney to bring back the medicine man. That night they got a big fire blazing in the camp. We sneaked quietly along a fence nearby and we watched and listened. The drums were beating and the medicine man was chanting and dancing around. It was exciting to see.

In the fall, when we were back at the Home Place, it would be time to round up the cattle from the summer range around Big Creek. My mother and dad sorted out the beef, which were to be sold, and kept back the cows and bulls.

When my mother rode out on the range, she'd often tie Tony and me onto a pack horse. She didn't have much choice as there weren't any baby-sitters nearby. She'd lead the horse until she found some cattle and then she'd tie it to a tree. Once she had the cows heading out, she'd come back and get us. I guess we cried and hollered a lot, but we did have our hands free so we could swat mosquitoes!

When our parents drove the cattle to Williams Lake to sell, it was a two-week journey because the cattle only travelled eight or nine miles a day. On these occasions they'd take Tony and me over to Charlie Bambrick's place. He and his wife were quite elderly, but they'd look after us while our parents were away.

I remember looking out across the creek one time, watching my dad and mother start out. I could just barely see them, but there was my mother, waving a white hanky at us. Imagine, going on a beef drive carrying a white hanky!

We sure had to do as we were told at the Bambricks' place. Mrs. Bambrick gave us way more oatmeal mush than we got at home, but we had to finish it all. We'd finally get it down, and right after that we had to sit on the pot. We had to produce something in that pot, too, even if we had to sit there all day! Between the mush and the pot, I never forgot Mrs. Bambrick.

Charlie would sit by the window sometimes, and I'd sit on his knee. He'd catch a yellow-jacket between his thumb and index finger and grind it up. He had skin like boot leather on his hands. Then he'd tell me to do it. I only did it once! We were always happy when our parents returned.

We'd stay at the Home Place awhile in the early winter, depending on how much hay there was to feed the cattle. We grew tame hay there, and it didn't always produce as well as the

Bob Fosbery watching Tony and Tex harrowing the garden with their horse Mike in 1931. The boys started young, learning to do ranch chores.

swamp hay. Sometimes we'd be at the Home Place until Christmas and sometimes we'd already be gone to one of the meadows by then.

My dad used a team and sleigh to carry our supplies from one meadow to the next. It was always so cold, sometimes down to 40 below. We'd bring the cats in a gunny sack and let the dog run alongside the sleigh. In the summer we'd even take the chickens in a box on the wagon, but we killed them off in the fall. My mother drove the cattle along the trail that had been broken by the team and sleigh.

We'd usually arrive at the meadow cabins after dark. My dad would get Tony and me and the potatoes inside as quickly as possible. We'd be crying from being so cold. My dad would put the potatoes in the middle of the floor and make us run around the pile so we'd warm up. In the meantime he'd light the fire and get snow to melt for water. He told me later that he had to give us a little "pop" on the backside with the bullwhip to get us moving. He'd have to go out and help my mother, and he didn't want us to sit down and freeze to death.

He'd light the gas lantern and go out to unhitch the team. Then he'd hook it up to a slip with a hayrack, they'd load it with

Eve Fosbery with sons Tony and Tex and friend Louis Vedan at his cabin in the Whitewater area. Bob's 1928 Model A Ford was the first car into that area.

hay, then take it out to feed the cattle. It was late when they got back. We'd have something to eat and go to bed. Tony and I slept on swamp hay on the floor, and Mother and Dad slept on a bed made of poles with a swamp hay mattress.

One winter at Dolly Meadow I had a wagon that my dad had brought along, even though the snow was too deep to really use it. One day I went out to play with it and it was gone. A few days later, on Christmas morning, we woke up and saw this beautiful Christmas tree—and my wagon with runners on it. I was so happy! Now I had a sleigh. Tony's present was up in the tree. It was a big green frog, probably made of inflated rubber.

Once when we were living in the Cooper Creek cabin, my dad brought home a dead coyote. There were lots of coyotes around because some calves had frozen to death, and the coyotes came to feed on them. My dad had shot several, but the one he brought back was a nice-looking one. It was frozen solid, so Tony and I put it on the sleigh, covered it with blankets and hauled it around for weeks. He was our pet dead coyote.

Another thing I remember about Cooper Creek was the owls. Dozens of owls sat in the trees around the cabin, hooting. My dad used to pack me outside at night to listen to them. I was so scared of their eerie sound.

My mother and dad were very strict, and Tony and I occasionally got in trouble with them. I still remember the three straps that hung in the living room at home. If we were bad, the only choice we had about our punishment was which strap we wanted used!

When I was six years old I had to start school. I was pretty happy with my life, but when I learned that I would be riding my horse the two miles to the Big Creek School, I thought it was even better. Hazel, Duane, and Veera Witte (now Veera Bonner) and Neville and Fay Blenkinsop were going there at that time.

Later on my parents started talking about sending me to a boarding school in England. I didn't have anything to say about it. There were other discussions that summer and the next thing I knew we were going to leave the Chilcotin and move to the Okanagan.

2

Growing Up in the Okanagan (1933-1942)

In early fall my dad made arrangements with Louis Quilt and his brother to hire a few others and drive the 200 head of cattle, my parents' saddlehorses, and a three-year-old work horse to Ashcroft. They were also going to take the team of horses and wagon. My dad let the other 40 head of horses go out onto the range to run wild. Most horses did that anyway.

My parents had packed up all our belongings. Gerald Blenkinsop came over and loaded our household goods onto his truck. We went in our Model A and stayed that last night at the Blenkinsops'. I looked out the window the next morning and saw Gerald's truck going up the long driveway in the snow. At the back of his load was the brass headboard of my parents' bed.

I don't remember much of the trip, but I guess we went down through the Gang Ranch. We had gone to the Okanagan that way before, to get some fruit and camp along the way. When we got to Ashcroft it was another world. It was warm and dry. We put up a tent beside the Thompson River near the stockyards.

The cattle and horses arrived, and the Quilts put them in the CPR corrals. My parents were gone quite a lot from our camp, making arrangements with the railway to ship everything to the Okanagan. One day they loaded the cattle into the cattle cars and the five horses into a boxcar with the Model A, freight wagon, furniture, chickens, cats, and dogs.

Tony and I were suddenly awakened that night and the tent was soon down and rolled up! My mother and dad picked us up and told us to be very, very quiet. They packed us up the hill, across some railroad tracks, and around some boxcars. We came up to our boxcar and my dad hauled us quickly inside and went back for the rest of the gear.

It was pitch black in there. We could hear steam engines puffing up and down the tracks nearby. My dad had told us to sit in the Model A and be real quiet. When he returned he stood at the boxcar door looking out through the crack. Finally there was a big bang as our car was hooked onto, and the next thing we knew we were travelling. I always said that Tony and I were probably the youngest hobos ever.

There were so many hobos in those days that the CPR had their own police. They weren't going to let anybody ride free on their trains. That's why my dad was being so careful.

We travelled until the next afternoon and finally stopped at Okanagan Landing at the head of Okanagan Lake. There was no rail line from Vernon down through the Okanagan Valley, so the freight all went by barge. The engine unhooked from the train and pushed all our cars onto the barge. There was a sternwheeler called the *Okanagan* that was going to take us down the lake. As soon as they untied us from the dock my dad said, "Okay. You can all get out now."

The crew on the boat was so nice to us. They took us into the dining room for pie and cake. It was a beautiful trip. It took about two hours to get to Bear Creek, which is a bit north of Kelowna but on the west side of the lake. There was an old rickety dock where they tied up the barge. It hadn't been used for many years. There had been a farm there at one time, which grew tobacco for making cigars, and it had been a very busy place.

When the *Okanagan* pulled away and left us there, my parents put us ashore on a blanket with some grub and proceeded to unload the cars. They got the horses off and tied them to some nearby trees. They had a hell of a time getting the big ramp over to the edge of the barge to unload the cattle. It was so close to the edge that there wasn't much room for a cow to come down the ramp, make the corner, and go along the barge and onto the dock. Those were wild Chilcotin cattle and they'd been penned up too long. When that door opened they raced down the ramp, hit the edge of the barge, and jumped straight into the lake! As soon as they hit shore some of them went straight through the fence and headed for the hills. My parents rode hard to try to herd them. They didn't get back until after dark, but they had managed to get the cattle rounded up and fix the fence.

There was a big house on this place at the mouth of Bear Creek. Catholic priests had lived there at one time and held church services in the chapel that was nearby. A Japanese family was now living in an orchard about 200 yards from the main house. There was a bit of a hayfield on the property as well as pastures for the cattle.

My dad had come down here for two reasons. It was 1932 and the price of beef was so poor that he decided it was time to make a move. Also, he was tired of moving from meadow to meadow at Big Creek, and he knew that the winters in the Okanagan were often mild enough for the cattle to rustle for their own food on the hillsides. There was lots of bunchgrass and open water along the lakeshore.

That winter was the worst in many years, with deep snow and very cold temperatures. My dad didn't have much money, so he had to buy hay on "jawbone," which is credit. Since he wasn't known in that area, he had a hard time making those arrangements. Then we all got the flu so bad that we couldn't even get out of bed to feed the cows and horses for a few days.

When we got settled I started going to the Bear Creek School, which was up the hill about a mile. There were eight kids in school and our teacher was Mrs. Daine. Her husband's name was Charlie and their daughters were Kitty and Doris. They lived about five miles down the lake and the girls went to school in Kelowna.

Mrs. Daine was a good teacher but very tough. I was left-handed and I wanted to write with my left hand, but there was no way she was going to allow that. I was forced to write with my right hand.

While we were in Bear Creek, the Depression got worse and cattle prices got worse. Between that and the hard winters, we had to cut down the herd. I remember my dad selling big two-year-old steers for $10 and feeling lucky to get it.

My parents decided to raise rabbits to sell. They started out with six and it wasn't long before there were over a hundred rabbits. Tony and I would cut alfalfa with a sickle for them to eat. When my dad went to Kelowna he'd take some to the local butcher shops, where he got 50 cents apiece for them.

My dad had put the Model A up on blocks. He bought an eighteen-foot boat with a Star engine and a driveshaft propellor system. He used it to go across the lake to Kelowna for supplies. One winter he worked for Sunrype, looking after their boilers, and he had many wild trips back from Kelowna on those dark snowy nights.

Tony and I enjoyed those years. We learned to swim and we fished for carp, trout, and suckers. We also did chores, which included carrying wood for the fireplace, bringing in water, and carrying out the slop water. These jobs were made much more difficult by the long flight of outside stairs up to the main floor.

My dad got me an old horse from the cavalry detachment at Kalamalka Lake. His name was Roy, but I often called him a rotten old so-and-so. He was gentle but very hard to catch. Almost every weekend I'd take a pan of oats out to the pasture and call him. He'd come and reach out and get the oats, but I couldn't slide the rope around his neck. Finally I'd catch him late on Sunday afternoon. I could only ride for a half hour before I had to turn him loose again because I couldn't ride during the week.

*Cowboy Tex riding his new
mare at Westbank in 1937. He
loved horses, just as his mother did.*

One day a fellow down the road heard about my problem. He said, "The next time you catch him just keep him in until I come over. I'll have something that will make him easier to catch."

He brought a double strap with a ring with a three-foot piece of chain attached. He put the strap around Roy's ankle and turned him loose. Roy started to run, but the chain banged into his legs and he had to stop. It was okay if he walked, but he couldn't run. I never had any more trouble catching him.

My mother had a new horse, too. He was a former polo pony and quite spoiled, but she was an excellent horsewoman and retrained him. We still had a few cattle in the hills, so we'd often ride out looking for them.

At that time my dad got to know Mr.Dole, "the pineapple king of Hawaii," who was also involved in gold mining. Dad started working for him and was away prospecting during the summers.

One day a strange looking car came into the yard. I learned later that it was a DeSoto. It was Mr. Dole and he had brought us a case of pineapple and a case of pineapple juice. I was impressed since we didn't normally have luxuries like that.

We did have apples and plums, and my mother had a big garden. Compared to the Chilcotin, it was a paradise as far as growing things went. There were also lots of deer in the hills, so we never went hungry.

Tony, Eve, and Tex Fosbery with their dog
Mickey at Westbank. Tex has loved dogs all his life.

We lived in Bear Creek for four years. When I was in Grade 4 we moved to Westbank. My dad rented twenty acres with an old house on it at the mouth of Sawmill Creek.

I was still interested in the Cariboo, so in 1938 when I was twelve my mother wrote to Queenie Blenkinsop asking if they could use me for a chore-boy. She replied that they could, so my mother arranged with some friends, Harry Parker and Howard Crowe, to take me to Williams Lake. They had an old Pontiac convertible with wooden wheels and were going prospecting around Horsefly. It was a three-day trip.

I started working for the Blenkinsops at the beginning of summer holidays. One of my jobs was wrangling horses. I sure liked that. I slept out on the veranda, and Gerald Blenkinsop would wake me up at five o'clock. I'd catch my wrangle horse and hop on bareback, which was the way I always rode until I was fifteen years old. I'd listen for the bells that were attached to some of the horses when they were turned out. Then I'd go and round them up.

Usually the mornings were sunny and cold. I wore jeans and a jacket and shirt, moccasins, and of course a cowboy hat of some sort. I liked to have the horses on the gallop when I brought them into the yard because I got a big thrill out of the sound of their hooves hitting the ground and echoing from the buildings.

I had them in by six o'clock. Then the teamsters came out and caught their horses, put them in the stalls, gave them some grain, and harnessed them up. By then Gerald would have breakfast on the table. The men had to be gone to the fields by seven o'clock. Queenie and Fay would get up then, clean up the dishes, and start preparing for lunch.

After breakfast I'd fill the woodbox. Gerald liked to have things tidy, so he had the woodpile a long way from the house. I'd bring three wheelbarrows full of wood each day and carry it in to the woodbox, which went right up to the ceiling. I also weeded the garden, got ice from the icehouse, and emptied slopbuckets. There weren't any bathrooms, so the women had pots under their beds that had to be emptied every day.

I learned how to handle a team of horses with a load of hay, and I painted fences. I was lucky to work there. It was a model ranch. I learned to work, be neat, and to respect other people's property. Gerald was one of the finest men I ever met.

Bill Fleming, a friend of the Blenkinsops, worked for them in the summer. I used to give him fifteen cents to buy me a package of cigarettes from Queenie's store at the ranch. Then I'd sneak off and have a smoke.

At the end of the summer Gerald gave me $5. That was a lot of money. I worked there for the next three summers.

That summer my dad was mining at Horsefly. He sent word to the Blenkinsops in the fall that he would pick me up in Williams Lake. I would be going to school in Horsefly until we returned to Westbank for the winter.

I rode in the back of Gerald's truck with the empty gas drums all the way to town. I stayed at the Lakeview Hotel that night. The next day two women picked me up, and when they finished their shopping we started out for Horsefly. After we passed the

150 Mile House the road became so narrow that the branches were brushing the sides of the car. It was like driving in a tunnel. I didn't know where we were going.

It was dark when we arrived at the Corner House. My dad was sitting there with a bunch of men. I was sure glad to see him. We stayed and ate dinner at the big round table. There were about a dozen others there, including the owner Bob Campbell. My dad was a man of social grace and charm. He was a real

Tex at thirteen years of age at Okanagan Mission, riding one of his favourite saddlehorses.

gentleman and had lots of friends. He use to say that he'd feel equally at ease dining with the queen as with his Chilcotin friends.

I was feeling pretty timid among all those people. I looked at the window and saw all these little faces pressed against the glass. Several kids were staring in at me, curious to see the new kid in town. I met them all when I started school. There was Leonard and Gilbert Walters and Maxine, Marilyn, Ray, and Jardie Webster. Some of them are still friends of mine today.

One of the girls I got to know at school was Phyllis Lincoln. I asked her to go to a dance with me one night. She said she would and I told her I'd pick her up that evening. She was staying with Mrs. Carson, who owned the store. Phyllis wasn't ready when I arrived so I sat in a big easy chair to wait. When I got up to go, Mrs. Carson said, "What have you done to my chair?"

I turned and looked. There was a big oily patch where my head had rested against the cushion.

"What have you got on your hair?" she asked.

"I don't like to tell you," I said. "It's three-in-one oil. I didn't have any brilliantine."

My dad and I lived in a little log house that is still standing today in Horsefly. Late in the fall we loaded up his 1937 Ford and headed for the Okanagan. We camped out the first night, and it rained so hard that the water was running through the middle of our bed. At daylight we drove south to Lac la Hache, where my dad made a fire in the rain and cooked bacon and eggs. It was a long trip on a road that was winding and full of holes.

After we got home I used my savings to order some riding boots. I sent a tracing of my foot to the Riley and McCormick catalogue, and for $13 I got a pair of boots made to order. They fit perfectly and were my pride and joy.

In 1939 we were at war with Germany. My dad said that he'd be joining the air force. He was going to make some extra money first by helping to build the barracks at the army camp at Vernon. There were going to be thousands of soldiers there.

We had lived in Westbank for four years, but now we moved to some acreage on Powers Creek at Okanagan Mission. I had a few different horses there and rode a lot with friends. I had a bike, too, and a bunch of us would ride to Kelowna for the matinee on Saturdays.

3

Cowboy Life for Me
(1942-1945)

I quit school in 1942 when I was sixteen and headed for the Chilcotin. Tony quit shortly after I did and went to work for a tinsmith in Kelowna. My dad was away in the air force, so my mother moved to Kelowna and drove for Pinky's Taxi during the war years.

My mother had made arrangements for me to go to work at the Cotton Ranch in the Chilcotin, so I jumped on a freight truck with my saddle, bedroll, and a few clothes. I was met at the Lakeview Hotel in Williams Lake by Charlie Moon, another rancher in the area. He drove me out to where the road turned down to the ranch, and Mr. Cotton met us there.

It was all pretty strange for me. I was the kid of the outfit and stayed with the rest of the crew in a big one-room bunkhouse. I had grandiose ideas of being a cowboy, but ended up weeding gardens, pruning raspberries, irrigating, and oiling harness. I found it hard to really put my heart into the job.

At the end of the first month, Mr. Cotton gave me a $25 cheque and told me I was no good to him. He said he'd take me to the Becher House[1] at Riske Creek, and I could catch Tommy Hodgson's Stage to Williams Lake, where I could get the bus back to the Okanagan.

By the time I got to the Becher House, I had decided that I was definitely not going home. I was determined to be a Chilcotin

Branding calves at Harry Durrell's Slee Place near Riske Creek. Jack Durrell is applying the brand while Stanley Perry and another fellow stretch the calf.

cowboy. "Little Mac" McKay and his wife Emogene were running the place at that time, and I knew them slightly. They were from Meldrum Creek and had two daughters and a son, Joan, Hazel, and Richard. They were pretty friendly people and suggested that I phone around and see if I could get a job. I phoned up Harry Durrell at the Slee Place. He said that he had a job for me if I could get myself up there.

When I arrived he asked, "Well, do you have a saddle?"

I said, "Yeah."

"Well, didn't you bring it?" he asked.

I said, "No."

He loaned me an old razor-backed horse and I rode back to the Becher House, seventeen miles away. I got my saddle and rode back. I went out on the roundup with Harry's son Jack and learned a lot of things. One of them was not to stand too close to the campfire. The jeans I wore were cowboy kings and they had a rivet at the bottom of the fly. In the summer we didn't wear underwear, so when that rivet got hot and I moved, was it hot!

The Durrells were good people to work for, but things were tough. We didn't have any fancy grub, mostly salmon and homemade bread. We slept out in the barn, which had just a pole roof with a bit of hay on it. Whenever it rained we got pretty wet. We'd hang our blankets over the sides of the stalls and hope that they'd get halfway dry by nighttime. They usually didn't.

When we finished the roundup Harry said, "Well, we'll be going haying before long, but I don't think you're big enough to pitch hay. I'm going to have to let you go."

There I was, out of a job again. Back to the Becher House I went. I phoned around and talked to Pudge Moon at Hillcrest Ranch. He said they could use a cowboy, so I went down there, and then out to Stack Valley where they ranged their cattle. I learned a lot more about cowboying and getting out on the range before daylight. We had to round up as many cattle as possible before it got too hot. They would stay in the bush in the daytime, and it was hard to find them or to get them out when we did. We usually quit about one or two o'clock in the afternoon to have a sleep, if we could. It was so hot. Then, after having something to eat about four o'clock, we'd ride until dark and go to bed. We'd get up early and out we'd go again.

After we finished the roundup and the branding we went back to Hillcrest Ranch where we started haying down on the sidehills below Sheep Creek with horses, pitchforks, and stacking-poles. I had the job of driving three horses pulling a big harrow. I was working about three miles south of the buildings. It was a tough job. I walked in seven inches of loose dirt. It was hot and dusty, with no shade anywhere. Of course I wasn't supposed to stop and sit in the shade anyway.

The cook at the ranch had a little boy, and one afternoon he decided to come with me. We took the horses back out and I hooked them onto the harrow. I worked for two or three hours. It was really hot that day, and I was dying of thirst. I don't know why I didn't take some water with me, but I didn't. I asked that little boy if he would go back to the ranch and get me a can of water. He said he would and away he went. It was a long way back to the ranch, and he was only about five years old. I was crazy to think he could do it. I watched for him all the rest of the afternoon.

I thought, "Maybe he isn't going to come."

I was so thirsty, so choked up with dust. Finally I saw this little speck coming closer and closer. I couldn't believe my eyes. It was him. He was coming along the dry old sidehill. Finally he came out onto the field. He got about a hundred yards from me when he tripped and fell down. All the water spilled out onto the ground! I've never forgotten his effort or my disappointment at not getting that drink.

When we finished haying in the fall, Pudge told Ed Garland and me to go and get some cattle out of Davis Meadow and then fix the fence.

Joe McLaughlin, another fellow who worked at the ranch, asked me to ride his little bay mare. He'd got her from the Toosey Reserve and she'd bucked him off a few times. I said I'd give her a try. Ed had her snubbed to his saddlehorn, I got on, and we headed out. We went over through Devil's Garden and along the lake. She was doing pretty good. Finally we decided that Ed would turn us loose. She started galloping and bucking, but I managed to stay with her.

About noon we found the cattle, kicked them out of the meadow, fixed the fence, and headed back toward the cabin. As I started over the top of a little hill, a breeze came up and blew my batwing chap against the bay's neck. She took off bucking wildly down that hill and onto the flat. She went round and round. Finally she got the better of me, but as I was going off, my belt and the one on the chaps hooked over the saddlehorn. There I was hanging upside down with her swinging me around.

Suddenly everything broke, and as I went sailing off, she kicked me in the back with both hind feet. Ed caught her and brought her back. I was hurting pretty bad, but after awhile I was able to get up and around. We got her snubbed up again and put a blind on her. I climbed on and rode her back to the ranch.

Later that fall we were laid off. By that time I had a horse of my own, so I saddled him up, put my blankets behind the saddle, and headed to the Becher House. I had to find another job. As it turned out, Little Mac McKay needed somebody to help him for the winter at the Becher House. I fed cattle, cut wood, and tried to keep the old house warm. That winter it got down to 40 below. I took the thermometer up to my room one time and it was 20 degrees below, Fahrenheit. But even in the harsh conditions, I enjoyed working for the McKays.

After Christmas I went on a beef drive with three other fellows, taking the cattle from Beaumont Meadow to Williams Lake. It was 35 below zero. We got to the Sheep Creek Bridge, which crosses the Fraser River. It could only handle 25 head of cattle safely at one time. I was following the first 25 across while the other boys held back the rest of the herd.

The cattle were trotting, and as they got to the middle of the bridge, it started swaying from side to side. It was growing worse and then I heard hooves pounding behind me. I turned to see 125 head of cattle coming toward me. They were trying to catch up with the first bunch. There was nowhere to go. The bridge was really rocking and my horse was losing his balance. I grabbed onto one of the cables on the bridge and held him against the railing with my legs. I figured that if the bridge went, my horse would go too, but I was going to hang onto that cable. Those cattle went trotting past me and the bridge held.

We got to Donald and Isabella MacKay's place at Four Mile Creek the second day. There wasn't room in the house for four extra cowboys to sleep, so Brownie Perry and I went out and slept in the hayloft. We buried ourselves in the hay with our blankets and managed to keep from freezing to death.

We finally got to Williams Lake the next day. We were up on the sidehill, which is a golf course now. The stockyards weren't ready for the cattle, so we waited for hours in the cold and snow. In the late afternoon we were still holding them on the sidehill. When we were driving the cattle, at least we could walk along for awhile to warm up, but here we could only walk in a big circle. It was tough walking in riding boots on a sidehill.

Mickey and Geneva Martin owned the Becher House at that time, and Mickey was with us on the drive. He said, "We're all getting terribly cold." Then he lit out on his saddlehorse toward town. We could see him going down the hill and across the old bridge, then along the road, past the livery barn, until he disappeared from our sight. We wondered where he'd gone, but it wasn't long before we could see him again. It was getting dark and he was coming back on a high lope. He came galloping up to one of the boys and gave him something and on to another and gave him something. Then he rode up to me and gave me something. I looked: it was a mickey of whiskey.

He said, "This is the only thing I can do for you to keep you warm."

We each opened our mickeys and got right into them. A few hours later, after we got the cattle into the stockyards and put our horses away, we weren't feeling any pain at all. Geneva came along and drove us up to the Lakeview Hotel. We were a pretty happy bunch and spent a great night in Williams Lake.

That winter Richard McKay—Little Mac and Emogene's son—was drafted into the army. He had to go to Little Mountain in Vancouver, so his dad and mother went with him to see him off. They were replaced at the Becher House by Wes and Mabel Jasper. Their son Delmer joined Hazel and Joan McKay there. We were feeding cows, cutting wood, and just having a lot of fun. Wes and Mabel were sure good people, and I got to know them very well. Later on, their home became my home whenever I was out of a job.

Lester Haller enjoys a smoke in front of the big barn at the Harper Ranch. Chilcotin cowboys often travelled about, working on different ranches.

It was 1943 and I hadn't been home in a year, so I went down to the Okanagan to visit my mother. My dad was in the air force, stationed at Rayleigh near Kamloops. He came home on leave while I was there.

He had got to know Sam Brookes, who owned the Powell River Pulp and Paper Company. Mr. Brookes had just bought the Harper Ranch near Kamloops.[2] My dad thought I might like to work there, so he'd made arrangements for me to do that if I wanted.

I went up to Kamloops with my dad and he introduced me to the foreman, Mickey Lowe. It was late at night. It always seems to be late at night when you do things in life. I wound up riding in the back of an old one-ton truck, heading out through the sagebrush, following the South Thompson River. I didn't know where we were going.

In the morning I woke up in the bunkhouse at the Harper Ranch. I spent from May to October working at the ranch. They had about 400 horses and a thousand head of cattle.

Mickey Lowe was a good foreman. So was Herb Wotzke, the foreman when Mickey was away. He and his wife Randie became good friends of mine. They lived in a little cabin down on the river. It was a great place to work that summer because we were all young guys, in our late teens. When I think back I pity the poor foreman who had to put up with us.

My old friends Bob Hutchinson and Delmer Jasper came down from Riske Creek to Kamloops that summer and we all rode in the rodeo. When it was over I asked Herb if Bob could stay on and work at the ranch. Bob and I were good buddies from the time when I'd worked at the Becher House and he worked for Mickey and Geneva Martin down at the Beaumont Ranch on the Chilcotin River. Bob was hired and that summer he and I bought a couple of horses and broke them ourselves.

In the fall we were going to be laid off. Herb was going up to the Cariboo to the Brookes' other ranch at the north end of Murphy Lake to pick up some equipment. He said that he'd haul our horses to the 150 Mile House. We arrived there and unloaded the horses. We didn't have much money, so we asked Mr. Zirnhelt, who owned the store and ranch, if we could sleep in the barn. He said, "Yes."

We managed to buy a little hay for our horses that night. The next day we struck off for Williams Lake, about ten miles away, on our green-broke horses. I got a job digging a ditch down on the lake for 25 cents an hour. Bob got some other job. We had our horses put up in Litzenberger's Livery Barn, but we weren't making enough money to keep ourselves and our horses, so we decided that we'd better get out of there.

We saddled up and headed out to look for work in the Chilcotin. We went down across the Fraser and up to the Becher House. There wasn't any work there, so we rode over to Farwell Canyon and down to the Pothole to talk to Charlie Hance. He was looking after all the steers for the Gang Ranch. He had 2,000 head of two-year-old steers on the north side of the Chilcotin River. He hired us both.

We rode for him until late in the fall. We'd ride out of the Pothole and down around the Junction. Usually we came back to the Pothole at night, but sometimes we'd stay out if we were in the high country along the bluffs above the river. There were corrals there, and a cabin known as Company Cabin.

One day Charlie said that we were going to move to Riske Creek and ride the area around Bald Mountain. He was breaking a big roan horse in his spare

Lester Haller standing tall in the saddle at the Harper Ranch near Kamloops. Cowboys worked hard, but also knew how to have fun.

time and had been riding it in the corral. He said that he'd ride it over to Riske Creek. We'd take a tent and camp there. There was about 40 acres where we could pasture our horses. Bob went ahead with a bunch of loose horses. Charlie was riding this big wild horse around in the corral.

I said, "How are you going to get out of the corral? Once you get off you won't be able to get back on outside the corral."

He said, "Oh, don't you worry about me. You just get going to Riske Creek."

I left at two o'clock with the team and wagon loaded with our sleeping gear and grub. On the tail end of the wagon was a hundred-pound sack of potatoes. I headed out and crossed the

Chilcotin River on the old bridge. There was a real steep pitch up from the bridge. It must have been about 35 percent. The horses had to get down and scratch to pull that wagon. I kept whipping on them and pushing on the lines to get them up that hill. It was a long way to the top and then a long way on over to Riske Creek.

I got there just about dark. Bob was waiting where we were going to set up camp. He had a campfire going and was sitting beside it. We put up the tent and made some supper, figuring that Charlie would be along anytime. It was getting really late and it was cold. We wanted to go out looking for him but decided that we'd never find him in the dark. Finally we went to bed, planning to get up early and go back along the trail.

Charlie rode into camp in the middle of the night. We asked him what happened, but he never really said much. What he did say to me was, "You should watch your load a little closer."

I knew what he was talking about. When I got to Riske Creek I saw that I'd lost the sack of potatoes. He said that they had come off right at the end of the bridge, going up that steep pitch. Poor old Charlie. It was bad enough to ride that horse out of the corral, but he had to ride it onto the bridge. It had never been on a bridge before with somebody on its back. He had got the horse across, but there was no way it was going by those potatoes. Charlie never did say how, but he finally made it. I felt really bad about that incident. The next day I went back with a packhorse and picked up the spuds.

We camped there for three weeks, about a half mile up the creek from Toosey Reserve. It was October, and one day it started to snow and didn't stop until there was a foot and a half on the ground. It was a pretty rough camp. We'd come back at night and light the fire. The tent would be half caved in with snow, and the blankets would be frozen. The water in the creek froze up so we were cutting waterholes for the horses and ourselves. We finally got finished and went back to the Pothole.

Charlie said he only needed one rider for the winter. Bob was a bigger and stronger man than I was, so he kept him. My saddlehorse was running loose on the other side of the river in a thousand-acre pasture on a steep sidehill. She had run with the other horses for about a month, and since I was on foot I had quite a time catching her. Bob and Charlie were out riding, so they couldn't help me. It took some time but I finally got her into the corral.

I had to ride all the way to the Gang Ranch to get my cheque. My horse sure didn't want to go. She wasn't used to going anywhere without having other horses along. Anyway, I beat her on over there and put her in the barn. I slept there as well. I picked up my cheque at the office in the morning. It was $30. I then rode back to the Pothole.

The next day I picked up my gear and headed up the mountain. The Durrells were still rounding up cattle on the old place at the northeast end of Bald Mountain, so I rode to their cowcamp. They needed another cowboy and got me to ride for them the rest of the fall. When we finished we went back to the Slee Place, their home ranch.

Harry Durrell wanted to drive his cattle up to Raven Lake and then push them over to Horseshoe Lake because it was good rustling there once the lakes and swamps froze up. When the snow got too deep, he'd bring them back to Raven and feed out the hay there. Then they'd go back to the Slee Place and eventually onto the spring range around Bald Mountain.

We had to cut a trail from Raven to Horseshoe Lake, so we got geared up with a team and wagon, tents, grub, axes, crosscut saws, and grain for the horses. Jack Durrell, Stanley Boyde, Fred Wycotte, and I headed out and spent the first night at Raven Lake. It was ten or twelve miles straight north to Horseshoe Lake and we were going to cut a trail wide enough to get the team and wagon through.

It was a tough show. We were able to work out of Raven Lake cabin for three days and then we moved our camp along as we went. We were working with axes and saws in fallen jackpine that was seven feet high in places. A fire had gone through there at one time and the second-growth pine was growing up through the blowdown. It was a real jungle.

It was Fred Wycotte's job to drive the team and wagon, put up camp, grain the horses, and hobble them so they wouldn't get away on us. It started to snow and we had to abandon the wagon. Fred built himself a big go-devil, which is a kind of sled. He moved our stuff along on it as we worked our way toward Horseshoe Lake.

Fred should have put a tongue on the go-devil because when he went down a hill it would run into the horses and just about break their legs. He'd whip them to make them go fast enough to stay ahead of it. Eventually they'd run off the road and the go-devil would hit a tree, and that's all that ever saved the horses.

We were on that job for a few weeks. Finally one afternoon in late December Jack said, "We'll be out on that meadow tonight or tomorrow. It's so miserable out here, let's try to get through tonight. There's a cabin there and we can stay in it."

We'd been sleeping in tents for so long and were tired of it, so we worked extra hard that afternoon. It was dark, but through the trees we could see a lighter area. Finally we cut the last tree and got everything out onto the meadow. Our saddles were on the sled, so we saddled up our horses and Jack, Stanley, and I started off at a high lope. It was cold and snowing and we were riding into a north wind.

Suddenly we heard a big yell behind us. It was Fred. Back we went. There was just a skim of ice over the swamp meadow. The team had broken through and had gone right down to their necks in mud and water. We got them unhooked from the go-devil, put ropes around their necks, and used our saddlehorses to pull them out. The team jumped and jumped and broke ice. Finally we got them up on harder ground. Poor things. They just about froze to death. It was dark and cold and that north wind was so bitter. We managed to hook onto the go-devil and pull it backwards out of the mud with the saddlehorses. We hooked the team up to it again and went around on higher ground.

Jack said, "I think that cabin is up ahead there. It's out on a little point in the swamp."

Pretty soon we saw this black blob and he said, "There it is."

By this time we were really shivering. We were soaking wet from messing around with the horses. We rode up to the cabin. Jack said, "There's a corral over there. Just take the horses over and stick them in there. I'll go in and get a fire going."

I put the horses in the corral. He was still banging away at the door when I came back. He couldn't get it open. It would only spring open at the top. Finally we got a pole and sprung the door, but it wouldn't let go at the bottom. We got our heads in and all we saw was the grey old sky. Part of the roof had fallen in and blocked the door shut. The other half, from the ridge-pole to the wall, hadn't fallen, so we had half a cabin. We climbed in through a window and broke up frozen chunks of dirt and wood and threw them out of the way. Finally we got the door open.

By that time Fred had come along with the go-devil, so we put the tent over the half of the cabin that didn't have a roof. Luckily the stove was in the side that had held up, so we were able to get a fire going. It was a big mess but we were out of the wind. We spent most of the night trying to get organized and get something to eat. Of course we had to feed the horses. We didn't have any hay, but we had lots of grain, so they got a good feed of it that night. We used our blankets to cover the team so they wouldn't freeze to death. Some of us stayed around the fire all night and never did sleep.

We worked out of that cabin and improved the road that we had skimmed through the day before. I remember that I lost my axe cutting a waterhole. I don't know what happened to it, but all of a sudden I didn't have an axe.

Jack said, "Well, you better do the cooking then as long as we're at Horseshoe Meadow."

I had a stove, and we had lots of moosemeat and rice, so I cooked them although I wasn't very good at it. We also ate dried prunes and apples.

When I got my cheque from that job there was a deduction of $2.75 for the axe. That was okay. I learned to look after people's tools better.

We got out of there and back to the Slee Place just before Christmas. Jack said, "We deserve a treat after that job. Tomorrow is Sunday so I'll get the Model A going and we'll go down to Hanceville for supper and a visit."

They served meals in Hanceville and had a real good cook, so it was going to be a nice change from our trail grub. We all had baths that night in the round tub beside the big heater in the bunkhouse. We were looking forward to our trip tomorrow.

Jack's car was a pretty little yellow coupe with a canvas top. It was parked in the lean-to attached to the bunkhouse. The next morning Jack got up early and lit the fire in the heater. He put the last tub of dirty water on to heat to put in the cooling system of the car. Water was hard to come by as it was a 50-yard walk through the snow to the creek, with a lot of ice to chop to keep the hole open.

Stanley and I lay in bed, waiting for the cabin to warm up. Jack had fed the horses and was happily whistling and singing as he got things ready for our big day. When the water was hot he rushed out with a bucketful and poured it into the radiator. He quickly started cranking the engine. He cranked and cranked.

My bunk was right next to the wall of the lean-to and I soon noticed that the whistling had stopped. I heard Jack swear. He came into the cabin with a bucketful of ice-cold water. He'd had to drain it out before it froze inside the block. Out he went with another bucketful of hot water, poured it in and cranked and cranked. Soon he was back, cursing internal combustion engines. He went out again, jacked up the right rear wheel, put a tire chain on it and poured hot water into the radiator. He got down on his knees and pulled the tire around and around by the chain. With the transmission in high gear, this procedure would sometimes start the engine. It didn't work for Jack. The air was blue with his cursing.

By this time breakfast was ready at the main house, so Stanley and I went over to eat. Jack continued working on that car. When we got back to the lean-to, Jack was beating on the car with the crank. I think that if he'd had a stick of dynamite he'd have blown it up.

I went to the corral, caught a saddlehorse, got a rope, and went over to the car. We hooked the rope to the front of it and the other end around the saddlehorn, filled the radiator with boiling water, and pulled the car around and around the yard. Finally it started.

We got to Hance's late in the day and had supper. We had to leave right after because the road wasn't ploughed and it was very slow going with chains on. By the time we got to Sawmill Creek the radiator was boiling. We stopped and wallowed down to the creek through the deep snow. We had an axe to cut a hole in the ice, but no bucket to carry the water. We took the little hubcaps off the car and made many trips up and down the bank in the dark. We finally got back to the ranch about midnight, glad that our Sunday outing was over.

We were going to move the cattle from the Slee Place to Raven Lake and then on to Horseshoe Lake. It was 52 degrees below Fahrenheit when we went out in the buck brush to round up those 300 head of cows. They were all humped up in the brush with a cloud of steam hanging over them. Did we ever have a time to get them to move. We took them three miles up to the yard to give them a good feed of hay before herding them on to Raven Lake the next day.

In the morning it was still terribly cold. We got the cows strung out on the trail. It was a long day. On the way out from Raven Lake a few days earlier we'd opened up a big haystack and thrown out a lot of hay. We knew that we wouldn't want to dig into a stack and feed 300 head of cows in the dark. I stayed at Raven Lake with Fred Wycotte for a few days.

I had told the Durrells that I was going home for a week at Christmas. When I left Raven Lake it was 40 below. I headed out wearing winter clothes, but not enough for that temperature. I also wore batwing chaps, which were soon as stiff as boards. My ears were cold right away. I'd rub them with my hand in my mitt and that seemed to make them feel all right. After awhile I forgot about my ears because the rest of me was so cold.

Finally I stopped and got off my horse. I rubbed my ear because it was kind of itchy. It felt like a piece of cardboard. They were both frozen solid and probably had been for a few hours. Not realizing that I should leave them frozen, I took off my neckerchief and wrapped it around my head. As they started to thaw out they swelled up into a couple of big lumps. We trotted for awhile and my ears felt like they were going to tear right off my head.

Eventually I got to the Slee Place. It was around suppertime, so I put my horse away and went into the house. I had a visit with Harry and Mrs. Durrell and Jack. There was nothing anyone could do about my ears. After supper I went out to the bunkhouse, but I couldn't sleep. I could hardly lie down. In the morning I looked in the mirror to comb my hair and was shocked when I saw my right ear out of the corner of my eye. It was swollen with water blisters.

It was still really cold outside. I was planning on catching a ride on Tommy Hodgson's Stage, which was supposed to be coming along soon, so I went out to listen for it. I had my neckerchief tied around my head. Eventually he came. He had two Indian women in the front of the old truck.

He said, "My God, man, you can't ride in the back with ears like that." He said to one of the Indian women, "You'll have to ride in the back. You can't let him ride back there with those ears or he'll lose them."

I got in front. I was lucky. That poor Indian woman was some cold. We did stop a few times to get warmed up, at the Becher House, at the top of the hill, and at Four Mile Creek.

Tommy said, "I've never seen ears that bad. I've been in this country all my life and I've never seen any like that. I hate to say it, but you're probably going to lose them. I'll take you to Dr. Atwood."

The doctor looked at them and said, "There's nothing I can do with them, absolutely nothing. All I can suggest is to put boracic acid on them. It'll dry them up."

I had a leather jacket on, and it was heavily coated with the juice running from my ears. When I got on the Pacific Stage Lines bus, people certainly took a good look at me. They didn't want to sit too close to me. They probably thought I had gonorrhea of the ear!

I went home and spent Christmas. My ears did improve considerably, so in a week I returned to Raven Lake. Of course I had proper clothing on the trip back. I stayed out there, replacing Fred Wycotte. There were 300 head of cattle to feed and waterholes to cut. The hay wasn't very good as it had a lot of moss in it. I fed and watered the cattle in the hospital yard by the cabin and put out three big sleighloads of hay for the rest of them. I did my best, but I never did get them filled up. They were always hungry. They would come around the cabin at night, bawling because they were so hungry. The days just weren't long enough. Many nights I'd be coming back in the moonlight to put away my gear, light a fire, and make some supper.

Some mornings after I'd fed the team I'd go to the hospital yard to cut a waterhole and find a cow with her head frozen into the ice. She had tried to go down the steps in the ice, fallen, and got her head into the waterhole. By morning the ice had frozen around her neck. I harnessed the team and then cut the ice. I hooked a rope onto the cow and dragged her out so the horses could get a drink.

I would often tail up the others in the hospital yard. Cattle get up with their back end first; so it was sometimes necessary to grab them by the tail to help them get on their feet. I'd help them down the steps to get a drink and then feed them some grain. Those that weren't able to get up, I hit on the back of the head with a double-bitted axe. After that I'd go out and do my day's work. It was a tough winter.

Harry came out every two weeks to see how I was doing. One day it was coming spring and I saw him riding out into the hayfield where I was loading hay from the stack. He was happy as always. I'll never forget how he looked. He had on a big old buffalo coat and a big cap down over his ears. He always wore moccasins and slip-on rubbers. He rode an old horse by the name of Steve. He carried a spur, but not on his foot because of the moccasins. He had it in his hand and he'd spur old Steve in the shoulder. There was always a kind of rough raw spot there. Harry came over and we had a little visit. He said, "I suppose you need some waterholes cut."

I said, "Yes. I sure do."

He took my axe off the sleigh and went over to a little lake where I was watering the big bunch of cattle. He opened up some waterholes and it wasn't long before he was back. Blood was pouring out of his rubber.

"God," he said, "I cut my toe with that axe. I'd better go up to the cabin."

That night I went up to put the horses away and do the other chores. When I stopped by the cabin to see how he was doing, he was soaking his foot in my frying pan. I kind of wondered why he didn't use the wash basin. When I went back an hour later he was frying beans in that pan for our supper. I always wondered how well he'd washed that pan!

We didn't have any first-aid supplies, so he wrapped my neckerchief around his foot and hobbled around the cabin, happy as ever. He was a great old guy.

I stayed there until March, when the hay was pretty well gone. Jack and a few of the other fellows came out, rounded up the cattle, and trailed them to the Slee Place. Then we went on down to the river, where I stayed until April.

It was 1944 and I had been thinking about joining the army. I told the Durrells that I was leaving. I went into Williams Lake and ran into Clarence Haller, who I'd worked with at the Harper Ranch. I told him what I was doing and he thought that he'd like to join up too.

Tony Woodland, a local businessman, was in charge of issuing train tickets and food vouchers. The government supplied these to anyone joining the army. We were supposed to report to Little Mountain in Vancouver in a couple of days. We caught the next train from Williams Lake to Squamish and then we caught the boat to Vancouver.

Clarence and I were billeted in the old Hotel Vancouver. We reported to Little Mountain, and when I stepped on the scale it registered 115 pounds! I was just skin and bones after that hard winter. They didn't believe that I was eighteen years old and told me that I could go to jail for a year if I was lying. The date was April 27, 1944, and it was my eighteenth birthday.

I went through the rest of the examination, but a few days later an officer informed me, "We've checked your birth certificate in Victoria and you are eighteen, but you aren't going to make it. You're not medically fit. Your right shoulder is underdeveloped."

I was so left-handed that I'd always favoured my right shoulder and arm. They wouldn't accept me, which was a great disappointment. Clarence got in and went overseas. I came back up to Ashcroft on a troop train and then on up to Williams Lake on the Pacific Stage.

I didn't know what I was going to do. I didn't have any money. Then I heard that Delmer Jasper was working for Percy and Rene Hance out at Hanceville, so I decided to go out and see if I could work along with him for my board. The arrangements were made and eventually I worked off wages to buy a horse from the ranch. I still had my saddle and my gear, so I had transportation again.

I started riding around the country looking for a job. I stopped at Leonard Palmantier's camp at the old Nick Carter place. He was cowboying for the Cotton Ranch at the time. He said that he could use me in a few days. I could stay there and they'd feed me until they were ready for the roundup on Tuesday. I lay around there for a few days and ate boiled deer meat. It made me so sick that for a couple of days I couldn't even get out of my bedroll.

I started to feel a little better on Sunday, so I rode up to see Delmer at the Jaspers' Milk Ranch. They had twenty head of unbroke horses in the corral. Delmer and Willie Johnson were going to drive them to Anahim Lake and they said they'd like me to come along. It sounded better than punching cows, so I rode back and told Leonard that I wouldn't be working for him and gathered up my blankets.

In the next couple of days we prepared for the trip. On the first day we trailed the horses through to Anahim Reserve. We couldn't find a place to hold them overnight there, so we went on past the reserve and found a place with a fence on each side of the road and about 60 feet in between. We checked the fence for a few miles up ahead and decided to camp there for the night. We figured those horses might try to come back the way we'd come, but they wouldn't go farther up the road, so we spread our beds out, with one on the hillside, one on the road, and one down below the road. After staking our own horses there, we each slept with one eye open.

The next day we got to Alexis Creek and rested the horses. Then we went on up to Mrs. Newton's place, where Delmer's sister June and her husband Jack Bliss worked. We stayed there for a couple of days and then headed off to Redstone, where we camped for the night.

All of those horses were supposed to be broke by the time we got to Anahim Lake, so we made a pact that every day one of us would ride a new horse. We'd rope one, snub it to a tree, saddle it up, and one of us would get on it. The other two would drive it along with the rest of the horses. There were some real stampedes! They had to be broke to carry packs as well as people, so we'd pack the horse that we'd ridden the day before. There were sure lots of wrecks in the jackpines.

On the day we left for Redstone, it was my turn to ride a new horse. I got on a big brown four year old. He never bucked but he ran a lot. I snubbed him to a tree while Delmer and Willie made arrangements to use Ed Lee's pasture. The other horses were grazing when suddenly something scared them. They took off and so did my horse. I only had one wrap of the rope around the tree. I was kneeling down and the rest of the lariat rope was caught around my feet and spurs. With only that one wrap I came flying into the tree really hard. When I was stopped by the tree, the rope just about ripped my legs off! Luckily the horse stopped, and only one boot was pulled off. Although it hurt pretty bad, it wasn't so bad that I couldn't carry on.

The next day we made it to Chilanko Forks. We holed up there for a day and then headed across country to Towdystan. It was really rocky country. We were on the trail about three days through there. The horses were getting trail-wise and sore footed, so they were much easier to handle. We finally got to Anahim

Lake and found a place to put them. We had spent seven days on the trail.

The Anahim Stampede was starting in a couple of days, on July 1. Delmer's dad, Wes, had followed us up in his Model A Ford and was going to sell the horses, as he knew a lot of the Indians there. He sold all but a good-looking brown workhorse that was a little lame and had been from birth. Nobody would buy him.

We hung around Anahim for a week and rode in the rodeo. There were 35 white people there and 500 Indians. They had come with horses and wagons, dogs and kids. There were Ulkatchos, Carriers, Chilcotins, and Shuswaps.

We were camped across the creek from Stan Dowling's store. He had a little pasture and we kept our saddlehorses with us there. One day while I was lighting the campfire, Wes went down to the creek to get a bucket of water. There were all kinds of Indians camped on the other side and lots of homebrew being passed around.

Wes didn't come back. I could hear the Indians hooting and hollering. I started thinking that they'd gotten hold of Wes and were beating the hell out of him.

I ran along the trail and down to the creek, looking ahead and across to the other side. There was somebody lying on the ground, and there were two Indian women beating this guy with rocks, but I could see it wasn't Wes. I was just about ready to run and jump across the creek when I saw Wes hiding in the bushes. He was watching this scene, laughing his guts out. He said he'd watched it from the start. That poor Indian buck was sure getting the treatment. They didn't kill him, but it looked like it was pretty close.

In the rodeo competition, Delmer won the saddle bronc riding and I won the steer riding, so we were real champions around there. We thought we were pretty smart, too. One day we rode double on Delmer's little pinto saddlehorse, bareback, over to

Stan Dowling's store. The pinto really didn't like that very much. We bought a paper bag full of oranges and came back out. Delmer got on first and then I grabbed the horse's mane and swung up behind him.

There were about 50 Indians sitting around the front of the store. One of them was Joe Elkins. Well, he took off his big black cowboy hat and sent it sailing out underneath that horse. The horse bucked, we landed in the dust, and he ran away. Our audience laughed and laughed.

"Look at the king of the cowboys now!" Joe said.

Every night there was a big dance in one of the old log cabins. Delmer and I would take off our riding boots, put on our moccasins, and head over there. There were Indians six feet deep around the cabin, sitting on the floor. The dust was just rolling up from that dirty old floor. Coal oil lamps at each end of the cabin glowed with a dim light. One Indian played the violin and one played the guitar. For a whole week of dancing the only tunes we heard were "You Are My Sunshine" and "The Anahim Two-Step." The old place was jumping continuously. We had a great time.

One night an Indian girl suddenly came up to me, put something in my hand, and ran outside into the dark. I went over to the coal oil lamp and saw that it was a rolled-up piece of paper. I opened it and read, "cowboy life for me."

Another night a drunken Anahim Lake rancher rode his horse into Stan Dowling's store and chased some Indian girls up and down the aisles, trying to catch one. Finally he gave up and rode out into the dark. His horse couldn't see and tumbled off the porch, falling on him.

When it was time to leave, Willie Johnson had sold his horse and Wes had sold nineteen. I had a little bay mare that I didn't want to sell, so it was up to me to take that unsold workhorse back to Riske Creek.

Delmer and I travelled with Thomas Elkins and his family until we got to the Newton Place, where Delmer sold his horse. I continued on with Thomas to the Anahim Reserve, and after that I was on my own with that crippled bay horse. The mare I was riding didn't really know anything, and the lame horse felt kind of lost and balked at being driven alone. He wasn't halter-broke well enough to lead, especially not with a green-broke horse. I had a heck of a time getting him from Anahim Reserve to Hanceville, beating him and myself half to pieces. I finally got to the Jaspers' late in the afternoon of the next day. My poor horse was played out, and I had run a stick in my eye.

I stayed with the Jaspers all summer, putting up hay at Paddy Meadow and other little meadows. In the fall there wasn't much left to do except hunt squirrels. Jack Bliss offered me a job on the roundup. He and June and I went riding up along the Chilko River on the summer range. It was cold and we were camped out all the time. I didn't have any winter underwear, but June loaned me a pair of her pajamas to wear under my clothes. I was very grateful.

Jack had an old Falcon-Knight car that he'd brought along for a chuckwagon. I think they only made seven of them. He liked to drive it better than horses. When we came back, after riding up there for a couple of weeks, Jack started talking about selling that car for $200. I didn't have $200, but I had a good saddle and outfit. I sold it off to the Indians until, with my wages, I had $180. I gave Jack the money and he gave me the car. I didn't have a driver's licence and I really didn't even know how to drive.

After that I was always looking for an excuse to quit my job so I could get in that car and go. I didn't have money for gas, but I just had to be on the road in that car. One day Jack and June were out riding and I was at the ranch with Mrs. Newton. She and I had a little spat and it was just the excuse I needed to quit.

I went out to the bunkhouse, gathered up my gear, and put it in the car. Jack had showed me how to start it with the crank. It had enough gas to make it to the Jaspers' place, and I'd worry about getting more when I got there. Mrs. Newton gave me my cheque, which wasn't very much because I'd gotten one shortly before and given it all to Jack. And I still owed him $20. I went out and cranked the car. I cranked and I cranked but that thing would not go.

That was one time in my life when I felt really small about asking for help. I had to ask Mrs. Newton if I could harness a team and get her to pull the car while I put it in gear and got it started. She was a pretty elderly lady, but she did all that for me and I was very grateful. Away I went to Alexis Creek, down through Hance's Timber, and down to the Jaspers'. I was a big shot now with a big car. I rolled in there after dark, out of gas.

Delmer and I cut firewood, shot squirrels, and fed cows. We managed between us to make some money on squirrels. We'd take them down to Rafferty's Store at Riske Creek by saddlehorse. We'd use the money to buy some gas in a can and pack it seven miles back home. Then we'd go for a drive in my big car. As it got colder, it got harder to start, so we always had a saddlehorse and a lariat rope handy. We'd put the rope on the bumper and snub it around the saddlehorn. Then one of us would ride the horse and the other would get the car going.

It was near Christmastime again, so I took the bus to my mother's place in Kelowna. I ran into Gus Connon, a fellow I'd known some years before. I talked him into coming back up to the Cariboo with me in January. My plan was to get my car, drive it back down to Kamloops, and get a job. It was wartime and I thought I'd probably get a job pretty easily.

We came up to Williams Lake on the bus. The timing wasn't right to go out to the ranch on the stage, so we rode out in the back of Harold Stuart's freight truck. He had a load of grain in sacks with a big tarp over it. We rode under the tarp on top of the grain. It was around 25 below zero, and we were sure cold when we finally got to the Jaspers'.

The Jaspers were all out at the meadow feeding cattle, so we went in and made ourselves at home. We got the fire going, and since there was lots of flour and baking powder, we ate hotcakes for the next few days. Then we started to get ready for the long trip south. There was a foot and a half of snow to shovel. It was about a hundred yards to the main road and we also had to dig a turnaround. In those days they only ploughed the main road occasionally with the grader.

No horses were around to help get the car started because they were all at the meadow with the Jaspers. There was a little hill down to a bridge and then another up to the main road. If that car was going to start it would have to be on that downhill or we'd be sitting in the middle of the bridge.

We shovelled snow for two days. Then we melted snow in a big tub on the stove. When the water was boiling we rushed out with it, closed the drain in the block and the radiator, and poured it in. We made sure there was gas at the vacuum pump and the carburetor. Then we pushed and pushed until we got the car to the top of the hill. It was just about dark. I jumped in and damned if it didn't start. We left it running while we gathered up our stuff and locked the house.

We got to Williams Lake and drove on through town. I didn't dare stop because I had no driver's licence. I had enough gas to get to the 150 Mile House. We got to the top of the 150 Mile hill and decided to turn the car around so it was pointing down the hill. We parked and drained it and walked to the hotel, where we spent the night in the lobby.

In the morning I took a four-gallon coal oil can to get some water from the creek. I had to chop a hole in the ice to get it. I poured the water into the old girl, gave her a push, and jumped in. We had a mile and a half of hill so we were sure it would start. I put it in every gear except reverse, but it just would not fire up. We were all the way down to the Sugarcane Reserve and it still wouldn't run.

The road was really narrow with only one track ploughed out. I looked ahead and saw a long procession of cars coming very slowly from Williams Lake. I said to Gus, "We'd better get this off the road and let all those cars go by."

We pushed it along into the Sugarcane road, which was narrower yet. Well, it was a funeral procession going to Sugarcane. They all had to stop their cars and help us push mine back to the main road so they could carry on to the graveyard.

I looked up the hill beside the road and saw an Indian fellow skidding logs with a team. I said, "That's the only hope we've got. We have to keep dragging it until it starts."

I went up and asked him to help us. He hooked on with the team and darned if it didn't start. We drove back to the 150 Mile House.

We had to have gas coupons in those days. I can't remember where I got them, but I had some, along with enough money to fill the tank. We left the 150 and drove as far as the 127 Mile, where I thought I'd better check the oil because it was burning a lot. It was nearly empty. I had to go in and bum some oil from the people at the 127.

We carried on all night, got to Savona, and slept in the car for a few hours. We were cold, tired, and hungry. One back window of the car was missing and there was no heater.

In the morning we gassed up again and headed up the road. Our journey of learning more about cars and driving wasn't over. We got halfway up the long steep hill and spun out. I had only one chain, so I put it on. The car wouldn't even move. I backed down and got the tire with the chain onto the ice. Luckily there was a little bare ground on the inside. The wheels on that side grabbed, and we finally made it to the top.

We got to Cherry Creek Ranch and had to stop and bum some oil from the Chinese cook. He didn't know, and we didn't know, what kind of oil should be in it. We might have put transmission oil in for all we knew.

We kept going and were more than happy to get to Kamloops. As we went down the hill into town, there was a breeze blowing from behind us. Well, that old car smoked so badly that the breeze, which was blowing a bit faster than we were travelling, blew in so much smoke that I had to stop because I couldn't see the road for the smoke. It was unbelievable!

By then I was sick and tired of cars. I drove it down into Chinatown, where I knew a fellow from when I'd worked at the Harper Ranch. I used to go to his restaurant, so I knew him quite well. I asked if I could park the car in his yard. He said, "Yes."

I was so glad to see the end of that thing.

Gus left and I tried to get back on at the Harper Ranch. They didn't need anybody in the wintertime, so I put my name in with the CNR. I said I'd do anything. I would have liked to wipe engines in the roundhouse because I'd be out of the weather. They said I might be able to get on the section gang. I checked with them every day. I had no money and nowhere to stay, so I slept in the lobby of the Leland Hotel. I could stay there from midnight until six in the morning. The rest of the time I wandered around the streets, visited a few people I knew, and tried to keep from freezing to death. I pretty well lived on a slice of toast and a cup of coffee a day.

Finally, after going down to the office every day for two weeks, they said, "Yes. There's a job for you up at Vavenby." That was the best news I'd heard for a long time. I got on a way-freight—a train made up of an engine, flatcar, and caboose—and when I got up there I saw snow like I'd never seen it before. It was piled ten feet high on both sides of the railroad tracks.

A German fellow met me and spoke to me in broken English. He said his name was Hans Stutts and he was the foreman. He took me over to the railroad bunkhouse, where there were six other fellows. It was just one room and the beds were "endo" (end to end) all the way around the room. There was a coal stove with a round top on it. Hans said that there was a store down below the tracks. I'd have to make my own arrangements to buy some food and then take turns cooking it on the stove.

I was the only one who spoke English except for the foreman. The rest of the men were Russians, Romanians, and Italians. It was tough because I could hardly communicate with anybody and I could tell they were talking about me. And because I was the youngest, I was always the last to use the stove at breakfast and suppertime. Lunch wasn't a problem because it was just a chunk of bread and a piece of cheese. I kept my grub in a powder-box under my bed. Eventually I got to know the people at the store and they invited me to eat with them. It was sure nice.

On that job there were two rates of pay. If you were 21 years old, you got 53 cents an hour, and if you were under 21, you got 47 cents. I wasn't 21, so I wasn't making much money, but at least I had a place to stay and a full belly.

We'd go out first thing in the morning and patrol the railroad track up to the Blue River section before the passenger train came through. Some days it was 30 below and we'd be riding on that speeder. There was a place where we'd take the car off the track and wait for the passenger train to go by. We would be cold already from riding 25 miles out in the wind and then we would have to ride 25 miles back to Vavenby.

We'd get warmed up and go out and shim the track, put in new tie plates, and shovel snow. They gave us some cork creations to strap on over our boots so we could stand on those slippery slopes to cut brush with a scythe from the sides of the tracks. We really earned our money. I quit three months later, which was the spring of 1945, and went back to work at the Harper Ranch.

My friends Herb and Randie Wotzke were still there, as well as Kenny Lindquist, his wife and kids, and Herb's brother Sam. It was kind of like coming home.

When haying time came along, Herb said, "We need some new workhorses, so we'd better start breaking some of these young colts. That would be a good job for you."

We had a big old gentle workhorse for an anchor horse. I started breaking these colts right from scratch and really enjoyed it. Those big workhorses seemed to have a different disposition from the smaller horses, although I still had some exciting times with them.

Tex sitting on his 1928 Falcon-Knight. He had no driver's licence and little money, but he drove it from the Chilcotin to Kamloops in 1945.

One day Herb said that he'd have to take my anchor horse and put it on another piece of equipment. "Probably one of the horses that you've hooked up several times will do to work with this other young horse. You'd better be careful though," he said.

So I was. I had them out on a ploughed field, pulling a big wagon and running them around for awhile. It took the edge off the greener one. Then we went back to the barn.

The crew was getting behind in raking hay, so Herb asked, "Do you think you could go out and rake some hay with that team?"

I said, "Yeah, I guess I could."

They used the old dump rakes in those days. Herb helped me get the horses hooked up to it. The hook to the dump lever on that rake was broken off. In order to keep the teeth off the ground while travelling on the road, I had to lift the teeth up by hand with the long lever and then put my foot on it. I worked my way carefully out through the gates, which Herb had opened for me. The hay rake was almost as wide as they were.

I got out into the field and gently let the teeth down and started off with my new team. Well, as soon as they heard the clatter of the teeth on the ground, they were something else to hold. That hay got raked pretty quickly. We went round and around for about an hour. I looked at my watch and saw that it was half-past eleven. I decided to get back to the barn while there was nobody around. I didn't want any noise while I was unhooking the team.

Tex enjoyed breaking horses. This was the first time out of the corral for this one at the Harper Ranch.

I got back through the gates and into the yard, talking to the horses all the time. They were pretty nervous. I parked off the road at the edge of the yard and gently let the teeth down. I kept talking to them, keeping a real tight line on them. Then I got off the rake. I unhooked the butt-chains and hooked them up on the britchen of the horse on the left-hand side. That was the most gentle one. I leaned across the tongue to unhook the butt-chains on the other horse. Just then somebody drove into the yard in an old truck. There was a big clanking and clattering and that was enough to excite them.

"Whoa. Whoa," I said. "Settle down here."

The horse that was unhooked completely from the rake made one little jump ahead. I jerked on the lines, but she'd jumped ahead enough that the tongue slipped out of the neck-yoke and fell to the ground with a crash. That was it. Away they went. As

Tex breaking a new workhorse to pull a dump rake.
This is how the rake looked before the big runaway.

Danny Seymour driving a buck rake at the Harper Ranch in 1945.
The rake picked up the hay on the forks and carried it to the stack.

soon as they did, I was right up against the frame of the rake. I knew that I had to get out from there or I'd get caught up in the teeth. There was no use hanging onto the horses. I threw myself backwards as I was being pulled down underneath, but I didn't make it in time. The frame of the rake hit me in the back, knocked me to the ground, and away we went.

I was rolling around in the teeth as the horses raced up the hill and swung around. I figured they were gone for good. Since one horse was hooked up and the other wasn't, the rake swung around with the tongue forced off to the side.

There was a big rock on the sidehill. One wheel hooked onto that rock and was ripped right off. The rake started being pulled "endo" (end over end), and that was good for me. I slid out the end where the wheel was gone. The horses continued to gallop up the road toward the yard. They didn't make the corner by the bunkhouse and hit the granary. That collision broke things up more. The rake came completely free of the horses, and away they went out into the hayfield. They just went crazy and tore everything to pieces.

I picked myself up off the ground. I had a long cut in my pants, right from the hip to the knee. It was like it was cut with a razor. I guess it was from a rake tooth. I didn't have any marks on me, but my back was sure in bad shape.

At lunchtime the boys went out and caught the horses. I was crippled up pretty bad, so Herb took me to town to the doctor. He looked at my back and told me to take it easy for awhile. I rested for a few days and then I felt better.

Herb and I eventually got those horses hooked up again. This time we put a heavy duty harness on them. We used a set of doubletrees with two four-gallon coal oil cans half full of rocks tied onto them. We each rode a saddlehorse. We had already put a "running W" on the team. This involved placing a hobble strap with a ring in it on each front foot. We ran a lariat rope down through the harness and through one ring, then brought it back up through another ring in the belly strap, then down again into the ring on the other foot. That causes the rope to form a "W." We did this on both horses, then took them out into the field.

I was holding the lines and Herb had the two lariat ropes snubbed on his saddlehorn. The horses had run away once, so that's all they knew. We just let them go and then yelled, "Whoa!" I pulled on the lines so they'd get the idea of what they were supposed to do. Of course they weren't going to stop, so Herb laid back on his horse, and the ropes to the hobble straps tightened. Those horses turned somersaults. They were all tangled up in the harness. We got them straightened out and repeated the procedure about three times. After that we could just whisper "Whoa" and they would stop. It was a good way to break a runaway team. I carried on and broke several more, but we made some changes so it was a little safer for me.

Later that summer I was riding in a rodeo and got bucked off. I hurt my left arm quite badly. Since I'm left-handed, I found it was inconvenient, though I was able to keep working. Each night I'd put cold water on my arm and by morning the swelling would be down. But it didn't get any better, so I decided to go to the doctor. They x-rayed it and found that there was a bone broken in the back of my wrist and the ends had started to heal over. They put it in a cast and I went back out to the ranch.

Irwin Kerr had just bought the ranch recently and he saw me with the cast. I thought, "Well, I guess this is it. I won't have a job."

We talked about it for a bit and he said, "Well at least you can ride. If you can saddle a horse, I guess we'll keep you on."

I rode all fall and into the winter. I'd have the cast changed every so often, but it wasn't getting any better. I was very fortunate that Irwin kept me on. There was no such thing as compensation or unemployment insurance, and I had nowhere to go. I did the best I could. I got so I could feed cattle by holding the fork over the top of the cast.

4

Moiling for Gold—and Other Things (1946-1947)

In January 1946 my dad wrote me from Trenton, Ontario, saying that he'd be discharged soon from the air force, where he'd been for the last five years.

He was an instructor of small arms and machine guns. He also had been on the coast patrol, watching for signs of a Japanese invasion. Two or three men, in radio contact with their superiors, had been stationed together in cabins along the Pacific coast. He had been at Bella Bella and at Alliford Bay in the Queen Charlotte Islands.

He wrote that he was going to the Forty Mile River in the Yukon. He'd be working for Mr. Dole. My dad had done some prospecting for him in California, Horsefly, Yukon, Okanagan, and Kettle Valley prior to the war. He said he needed two men to work with him. He'd also contacted my brother Tony, who at that time was first mate on the *Pentona*, one of the tugs on Okanagan Lake.

Dad said he'd be in Kamloops on May 6. If I was there, he'd take me. I was there. I sure hated to tell Irwin Kerr that I was going to leave. I was just getting so I could do something again. I guess I burned a bridge behind me there, but it was an opportunity I had to take.

Dad had written, "The grub will be poor, the pay will be poor, the hours will be long, and the mosquitoes will be hell!"

Both Tony and I went. He arrived in Kamloops with a brand new 1946 half-ton Ford supplied by the company. It was loaded with picks and shovels, pumps and hoses, and other prospecting gear. We drove to Vancouver, where he took us to Jones Tent and Awning. He bought us new sleeping bags, packboards, "bonedry" pants, coats, and hats. It was an exciting time.

I had only been in Vancouver once before, when I'd tried to join the army. We would be travelling north on the *Princess Louise* from Vancouver to

Brothers Tex and Tony Fosbery in Vancouver, on their way to a new life in the Yukon. "City duds" were a far cry from their cowboy clothes.

Skagway, Alaska, but we had a few days in the city while the ship was being loaded. When the ship pulled away, it was nine o'clock at night. The sun was low in the sky, shining on the water, as we left Vancouver and headed up the Inside Passage. It was all beautiful: the ship, food, dining room, and staterooms.

We stopped at several places along the way—Bella Bella, Prince Rupert, Ketchikan, Petersburg, and Wrangell. When we stopped for several hours at Juneau, we went ashore, and my dad took us to the Baronoff Hotel.

We noticed that people didn't use paper money there, just silver dollars. We cashed in our paper for silver. It felt pretty good to have a big pocketful of silver dollars. It was a wild town.

Bob Fosbery and his new 1946 Ford pickup, which came up from Vancouver to Skagway on the ship. It then rode on a rail car to Whitehorse and on a barge down the Yukon River to Dawson City.

We were able to go in the bar and have a drink. We took a taxi back to the ship. The young driver said that he was going to the Yukon someday and that we might see him there, which we did.

The ship continued its journey to Skagway, and we arrived in the afternoon. There was a mile-long dock across the mud flats. We tied up at the end of it and walked along to the White Pass train station. All the freight had to be unloaded, moved uptown, and loaded into the boxcars and flatcars. Most of the gear was pickups and fuel.

We stayed in Skagway that night, and by next morning the train was loaded. We couldn't believe what a tiny train it was—a narrow gauge with three little steam engines and eleven cars. We headed up the White Pass through the fog, snow, and ice. Those little engines were just spinning away. Sparks were flying off the wheels because it was such a steep incline. We were going so slow that Tony and I stood out on the tail end of the train, dragging our fingers along the ice of the glaciers. They were so close that they had to be continually chopped away so they didn't creep down over the track.

We came to Dead Horse Gulch, looked down, and there we could see the bones of thousands of horses. They had died there during the gold rush of 1898, struggling up the mountain as far as they could and then dying of overwork and lack of food.

Dead Horse Gulch on the White Pass Railway line from Skagway, Alaska, to Whitehorse, Yukon. "We could see the bones of thousands of horses that had died during the gold rush of 1898."

We continued on to Lake Bennett, where we had lunch at a little restaurant and looked at the church. They watered up the engines on the train, and we went on to Whitehorse. It was late in the afternoon when we arrived. Dad put us up in the Whitehorse Inn. The next day we unloaded the pickup and other equipment off the train.

My dad went down to the White Pass Station to see when the boats would be running to Dawson City. The first one was supposed to go between May 16 and 20, but it hadn't gone because the ice wasn't yet out of Lake Laberge. The rivers were open but not the lake.

Dad made arrangements to rent a little trailer on the outskirts of Whitehorse. It was about seven feet wide and twelve feet long. There were three bunks in it and a stove. We batched there while we waited for the steamboat.

In the meantime, he wasn't going to have us living the life of Riley. He got us a job digging a basement for a U.S. soldier who had decided to stay in the Yukon. My dad volunteered our labour

Tex at the trailer at Whitehorse while waiting for the ice to go out of Lake Laberge. The trailer was seven feet wide, twelve feet long, and barely high enough for him to stand up in.

and we dug for several days with picks and shovels and wheelbarrows.

There were about 11,000 American soldiers still in Whitehorse, even though the war was over, so it was one wild town.

One day while we were working we saw a little blue car go by in the dust. It was a Model A coupe pulling a little blue trailer, and we could see that the licence plates said Albuquerque, New Mexico. We were surprised to see it way up in that country. That night after work and supper, Tony and I walked downtown. We went to the docks where all the steamboats were tied up. There was always lots of activity along the river.

We saw the blue car down past the docks. The driver and passenger had a camp on the riverbank, so we went over and talked to them. One was an old fellow on crutches. He said that they'd come because he had a claim on Hunker Creek, a few miles out of Dawson City. He'd got flooded out years ago just when he got to bedrock. He knew there was good gold on the bedrock. He had told the other fellow that if he'd drive him up here, he'd give him the claim. The driver was a fat little guy with red hair and beard who had been a U.S. Marines pilot in the South Pacific. His name was Les Steinhelber.

Les had decided not to ship his Model A and trailer on the barge down to Dawson City. He was going to build a raft and float it down. In a few days they had a raft built. One night they went uptown for supper and when they came back, the raft was gone. They'd just had a light rope holding it to shore. The river had come up, the rope had broken, and the raft had floated away.

They ended up travelling with us on the *Casca*, which left for Dawson on June 1. We went from Whitehorse to Lake Laberge, crossed it, and then went down the Thirty Mile River to Hootalinqua. There it joined the Teslin and really became the Yukon River. In the old days the river between Whitehorse and Lake Laberge was called the Lewis River.

We travelled all night. At that time of year it was light 24 hours a day. We stopped at the big woodpiles along the river. We needed lots of wood to fire up the steam boilers. When we arrived at Minto the next morning, we pulled into a big slough. There was an Indian village there. A lot of freight was unloaded and wood loaded on.

Tony and I walked around the village. The poor husky dogs were tied to trees, almost starving to death. I guess there was no game and nothing for them to eat. It was a pretty sad sight. The Indians were damn hungry, too. I remember that those Indians had lines drawn on their foreheads and around their noses. I believe they were of the Northern Tutchone Band.

Soon we were ready to go again. Tony and I were standing up by the wheelhouse. The captain's window was open right above our heads, and we heard the bells ring for reverse. The boat backed halfway across the big slough. Then we heard the bells ring to go ahead, but nothing happened. The bells rang harder and faster to go ahead, but the boat was still in reverse. It was getting pretty close to the other side of the slough.

Tony and I ran the full length of the boat to the stern, about 200 feet. From up on the deck above the big paddlewheel, we watched it hit the shore. The paddlewheel started pulling the boat right up onto the beach. The paddle was ripping apart and the rudders were breaking up. The captain was screaming. Then the engines stopped. Silence.

There was a bit of current in the slough, and the bow slowly swung downstream. The next thing we knew we were floating again. The boat had slipped off the shore, and we were drifting toward the main river, hugging the shore. The overhanging branches, or sweepers, were ripping off the boat's railings and smashing its windows. The captain yelled for one of the deckhands to jump overboard with a rope and snub the boat to a tree. Finally, just before we swung out into midstream, they got it secured. Lord knows where we would have gone if we'd got into the main river with no control.

It wasn't long before the hands were over the stern, fixing the paddle. In about a day's time we were underway again. It was sure an interesting experience for us.

We stopped in several places along the way. As we unloaded some freight at Fort Selkirk, we saw the *Keno* go by, pushing a barge on its way to the mouth of the Stewart River. There the *Casca* would take over the barge, and the *Keno* would continue on up the Stewart to Mayo. The *Keno* was smaller, made especially for smaller rivers. Its job for many years had been hauling silver ore from Mayo to the main river. Once there, the bigger boats picked up the barges and pushed them upriver to Whitehorse. The ore was then shipped by railroad to Skagway, transferred onto the big ships, and taken to the smelters in Oregon. Those sacks of ore were handled five times, and millions of tons travelled that way over the years.

It was a great experience to be in Fort Selkirk. The population was about 300 at that time. There were trappers, miners, Indians, RCMP, and Hudson's Bay people. There were no roads, so the

Switching the barge from the Keno (top) to the Casca at the mouth of the Stewart River. The Keno was a smaller boat, able to travel on smaller rivers. It was used for many years to carry silver ore from Mayo. The barge (centre) loaded with fuel, trucks, and other supplies going down the Yukon River. There was no road to Dawson City in 1946, so the river was its lifeline. The steamboat Casca (bottom) pushes the loaded barge down the Yukon River from the mouth of the Stewart River to Dawson City. The boat stopped at the big woodpiles along the way to take on more wood to fire up the steam boilers.

Celebrating the 50th anniversary of the discovery of gold on Bonanza Creek near Dawson City. A familiar landmark at Dawson is the slide on the mountain.

town depended on the river traffic in the summertime. In the old days there had been horse-drawn stages between Dawson City and Whitehorse, and Fort Selkirk was one of their stopping places.

We continued on to the mouth of the Stewart. At one time there were a thousand people living there. It's where Jack London wrote a lot of his stories. He'd wintered there his first year up north.

Around midnight on Sunday the whistle on the *Casca* started to blow. Everybody jumped up and ran to the railing to see what was happening. We came around the corner and there was Dawson City. We swung around in the river and nosed upstream into the big docks. There were lots of docks there. As we were tying up we looked down from the railing. Bands were playing. People were waving and cheering. We noticed that a lot of them were old people with white hair. They were a happy-looking bunch. The gangplank went down, and we went ashore. Everybody came and shook our hands and wanted to talk to us. They hadn't seen a steamboat since the previous September.

In those days there weren't any roads into Dawson. There was just a trail across from Tok Junction, Alaska, to Boundary and Sixty Mile. You could drive on it in summertime, but it was marginal, as I got to know later on. That road is now called the Top of the World Highway.

Dawson City was wide open at night. We could go into the bars. We thought that was pretty good because we were both underage.

As we went up to the Regina Hotel from the dock, Les Steinhelber and the old fellow were walking ahead of us. There were some young Indian fellows coming down the sidewalk. They walked on by, but behind them was an old Indian lady. When she got right in front of the old fellow, she stopped and let out a yell. He threw down his crutches on the sidewalk and they grabbed each other. They hung onto each other and cried and laughed. It turned out that she was his woman from many years ago, when he was a young man and she was a young girl.

We got a room at the Regina Hotel, slept awhile, and went back to the docks later in the morning. They were starting to unload the pickup and other gear off the barge. We noticed that Les wasn't saying too much as he picked up his Model A and trailer. Later on we found out the reason. That old fellow had promised him a claim on Hunker Creek, but there was no claim. He had told him the night before that he just wanted to come back to Dawson one more time before he died.

But Les was soon his happy self again, and he did fairly well in the next few years, prospecting and mining.

We rented a house on Fifth Avenue in Dawson for $15 a month. It was our headquarters, a place for my dad to stay when he came to town for supplies. We left some of our personal stuff there and headed down the river.

My dad had bought a boat in Whitehorse. It was a sixteen-foot boat with a 25 horsepower Johnson outboard motor—two cylinders with a rope start. Trying to start it was a real good way

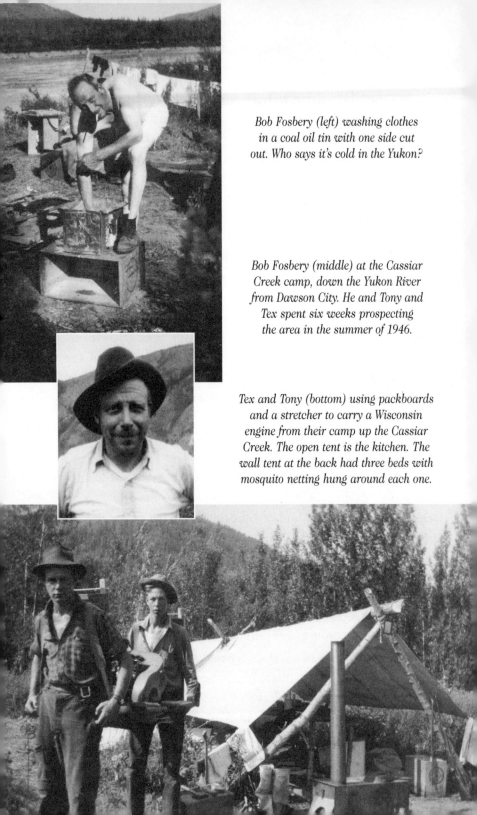

Bob Fosbery (left) washing clothes
in a coal oil tin with one side cut
out. Who says it's cold in the Yukon?

Bob Fosbery (middle) at the Cassiar
Creek camp, down the Yukon River
from Dawson City. He and Tony and
Tex spent six weeks prospecting
the area in the summer of 1946.

Tex and Tony (bottom) using packboards
and a stretcher to carry a Wisconsin
engine from their camp up the Cassiar
Creek. The open tent is the kitchen. The
wall tent at the back had three beds with
mosquito netting hung around each one.

to get blisters. The boat was loaded to the gunwales with pumps, picks, shovels, and other prospecting gear.

Tony and I didn't know where we were going, but my dad did. We went 50 miles north down the Yukon River to Cassiar Creek, where we set up camp and spent the next six weeks.

We took turns doing the cooking, even though none of us particularly liked it. My dad said that anyone who criticized would have a steady job cooking. One day I cooked rice for supper and it was pretty burnt. Tony took one look at it and said, "Jesus Christ! Burnt rice!" After a moment he added, "Just the way I like it."

We chopped out a trail about a mile and a half up the creek from our camp. When we found outcrops of bedrock, we started putting down shafts. There were logs across the creek that we used for bridges. We packed a Wisconsin engine up there, along with cable, blocks, and other equipment. We made up a kind of stretcher to carry these things. We shoved the handles through the bottom straps of the packboards on our backs. One of us walked ahead and one behind with the loaded stretcher in the middle. It worked fine on the level, but on uneven ground or across logs it was something else. We were trying to balance the load while I tipped one way and Tony the other. We fell down many times. The air got pretty blue.

We put down several shafts but didn't find enough gold to make it worthwhile. One day my dad said, "Well, that's it. We're leaving here and heading over to Sixty Mile."

The company had another operation there. We went back up the river to Dawson City and then 60 miles to the west. It is a beautiful drive now into Alaska, but it was a terrible ten-hour trip for us. There were mud holes and steep draws and gullies. We had to put chains on the tires even where it wasn't wet because it was so steep. Eventually we got to Sixty Mile, down to the old Holbrook Camp. The Holbrooks had built a dredge and mined there years before. There were some bunkhouses and a cookhouse, so it became our camp for awhile.

We had a cook there who we called Jello Jack because he always made jello for dessert. Every night after work, my dad, Harry Sogoff, Joe Walsh, Tony, and I would have a drink of 150 overproof rum before supper. One night I went over to the cookhouse and opened the door to a big cloud of smoke. There was Jack passed out on his burning mattress. He'd been into the rum. I rushed in and threw a bucket of water over him. He came up cursing off that bed. He ran to the table and grabbed a big butcher knife and came after me. Fortunately for me he didn't catch me. My dad fired him and told him to get out of camp.

There was a lot of ground in that area that had never been mined, and the company planned to drill it to see what was there. We had an old Keystone steam drill, which travelled under its own power as long as it had steam up. When we wanted to drill, we'd put up the derrick and raise and lower the drill stem on an eccentric system that's too hard to explain here. Joe Walsh taught Tony how to operate the drill.

The company also had a two-ton Holt cat. It was the first time I ran a cat. I learned a lot quickly. It had a crank on it, and if I buried the front end, the crank would always go down in under the mud.

One day my dad brought an old man with him from town. He was 81 years old. He didn't have a tooth in his head or a hair on his head. He smoked a corncob pipe, and every time he took his hand off it, it would turn over because he didn't have any teeth to hold it.

"What did you hire him for?" I asked.

My dad said, "He's going to show you how to work in this country. He's not going to work. He's just going to travel around and show you boys how things are done in the Yukon."

His name was Charlie Stone. He had at one time been the biggest horse-freighter in the Dawson and Mayo areas. He had 22 teams of horses and freighted all the mining equipment from

Tony oiling the sheave on the top of the 35-foot-high drill derrick.

A little oil on the wood helped get the steam up and the smoke black.

The Keystone drill travelled under its own steam power, with assistance from the cat in difficult areas. It covered a lot of ground, drilling test holes in the search for gold around the Sixty Mile area in 1946.

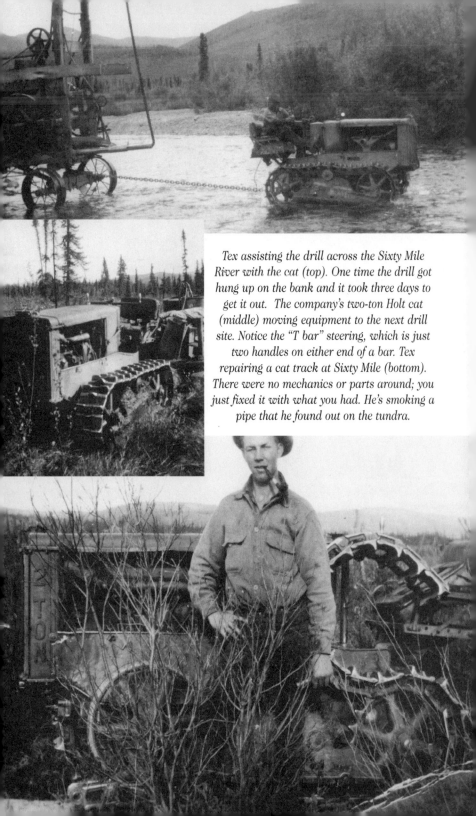

Tex assisting the drill across the Sixty Mile River with the cat (top). One time the drill got hung up on the bank and it took three days to get it out. The company's two-ton Holt cat (middle) moving equipment to the next drill site. Notice the "T bar" steering, which is just two handles on either end of a bar. Tex repairing a cat track at Sixty Mile (bottom). There were no mechanics or parts around; you just fixed it with what you had. He's smoking a pipe that he found out on the tundra.

the riverboats up the creeks. He also hauled wood and had a big hay ranch at Mayo, where he used to winter a lot of his horses.

He certainly taught me a lot. I'd get stuck with the cat and it would look hopeless to me. He'd show me all kinds of tricks with a piece of cable, even though I didn't have a winch. There are things that I still use that I learned from Charlie Stone.

We travelled miles all over the country with that drill and the cat. My dad and Joe Walsh would lay out a pattern and we'd put down holes every hundred feet. Joe had been in the Yukon most of his life, and he knew the Sixty Mile country well.

We slept under the drill a lot in the summertime, or under a tarp. We cooked all our meals with steam because we had lots of it. It was too hard to start a fire in that tundra. It was just moss with ice under it, so it was pretty hard to get a good cooking fire going. There was always a fire in the boiler of the drill in the daytime. We used to stuff the end of the hose down under the moss and put a big pot of meat, beans, or vegetables in there, turn on the steam, and let it cook. The pot was all covered up with moss and the steam would come up under the pot. It worked out pretty good.

Harry Colley was another of our cooks. He was also the founder of the Calumet Mine at Keno City in the Yukon. When my dad brought him out to where we were working, he almost fell out of the truck. Dad said he'd be good once he sobered up, and he was.

We came in from work one night and saw he had made blueberry pie. We poured canned milk on it and dug right into it. After a few mouthfuls I noticed that some of the berries tasted kind of flat. I looked more closely and saw that they weren't berries. A good percentage were rabbit manure. Harry had combed the berries from the bushes and hadn't separated them from the rest of the pickings. It was still a luxury, rabbit "berries" and all!

We travelled up to the mouth of Miller Creek, and by fall we were up around the mouth of Bedrock Creek. By that time everybody had gone back "outside" on the last boat, which left on September 15. The weather was getting pretty nippy. Only Dad, Tony, and I had stayed, so there were just the three of us doing the drilling and moving.

One night we were up in the cabin at Bedrock Creek, which was two miles up from the drill. It had snowed all day and started to freeze that night. We had supper and went to bed. The fire was crackling away and we were just about asleep. My dad asked, "Which one of you fellows drained the drill?"

Of course a steam drill uses water, and if it froze up it would bust all the flues and we'd be out of business. I couldn't remember doing it, and Tony couldn't remember doing it. We got up and lit the coal oil lamp. Dad put two matchsticks behind his back. He said, "Whoever gets the short one has to go down and make sure it's drained."

Well, I pulled the short one, so I had to put on all my clothes and go out. It was pitch black. My boots made a crunching sound in the snow as I walked along the creek through the willow brush. I had gone about a quarter of a mile when I thought I heard some yipping in the hills behind me and off to my right. Then I heard it again. It was getting closer. Soon I heard a lot of yipping and it was getting really close. I figured it must be wolves and they were on my trail.

I hurried faster, but they were getting closer. There were no trees to climb. I'd never heard of wolves attacking anybody, but it sure sounded like they were after me. I had nowhere to go. I remembered hearing that if you pretend you're dead, nine times out of ten no animal will bother you. I threw myself down in the snow and listened to them running toward me.

Then I realized that they weren't on the trail that I was on. They were across the creek in the willow brush. I could hear their feet on the crusty snow as they went by. I didn't know what they were chasing. Now I was wondering if they were going to wait for me down the trail somewhere. I had a long way to go yet. I was sure sweating. I didn't want to go but I had to. And to finish me off, when I got to the bloody drill I found that it had been drained.

Another night we had just gone to bed when we noticed a flashing light on the window. We went outside and saw one of the most spectacular displays of northern lights. Many shades of green were sweeping back and forth across the sky, making a swishing sound. We stood there for a long time in our underwear with the temperature at ten degrees below, Fahrenheit.

We moved out of Bedrock Creek shortly after that, back down to the Holbrook Camp. There was nobody there but us at that time of year. The last time he was in town, my dad had arranged a date for a six-wheel-drive army truck to come from Dawson to pick us up, along with the cat and all our gear. We were starting to worry about the Yukon River freezing because the ferry was pulled out when the river got too much slush ice running.

We were waiting around for a few days, and one morning my dad said, "You know, we borrowed some stuff from the boys up on Miller Creek. That would be something for you to do today. You can take the cat and the go-devil and take it up to them."

Tony rode on the go-devil and I was on the cat and away we went. It was about five miles up there. We arrived around eleven o'clock.

One of the men was a big Swede by the name of Ole Medby, and the other was Ovi Semsmo, a Norwegian. They were partners and had been mining there for quite a few years. Then would put down a shaft to bedrock, drift along it, creating a tunnel, and bring up all their material to the surface. Then they put it in a big dump on the side of the hill. In the springtime, when the water was running again, they'd wash their dump, and that's the way they got their gold.

They were glad to see us. We unloaded the pipe, drill casing, and crosscut saw that we'd borrowed from them. They said, "Come on in and we'll have a hot rum before you go back."

They had all their Christmas liquor and grub for the winter. It would be spring before they'd take their dog team and go out to Dawson. We went in and had a hot rum. It tasted pretty good. Ovi said, "You'd better have another one."

The next thing we knew, between the four of us we'd finished the whole bottle of Demerara rum. We said we'd better get going.

"Oh, you better have lunch," Ole said.

While we were having lunch, Ole said, "Well, if you have the cat here, we've got a boiler down at the creek that we'd like to move up to the shaft on the hillside above the cabin. Would you pull it up there with the cat?"

I said, "Sure. We'll do that."

Right after lunch we had another hot rum, and then I took the cat down, hooked onto the boiler, and dragged it up to the shaft. There were real thick willows around there, about ten to twelve feet high, and there was a winding, twisty trail through the willows.

Ovi said, "I always wanted to run a cat. Could I run your cat back down to the cabin?"

I said, "Sure."

I should never have agreed to it. The cat was a funny old thing. It had two brake pedals on the right side and a foot clutch pedal on the left side. The gearshift was on the right, alongside the seat, and it had a T-bar for steering. Ovi got onto the cat, and I put it in high gear and opened the throttle. I told him, "When you go, just take your foot off the clutch, and when you want to turn, just push on one side of the bar and pull on the other."

He took his foot off the clutch and away he went. That thing just took off. It could go five miles per hour. It tore off into the willows and he literally disappeared. The willows were going down in front of him and popping back up behind him. He was roaring along the sidehill. All of a sudden we couldn't see or hear him and he hadn't gone very far.

We ran through the willows and there he was. He hadn't gone 60 feet. The cat was lying over on her side and the water and oil were pouring out. It lay there gurgling, still running. Luckily Ovi had been thrown right out of the seat. He was lying down in the willows with not a scratch on him.

We sobered up pretty quickly. It was getting late in the day, and we had to get the thing back on its feet. We shut it off. We got a big pole and a chain and hooked it on the track. Then we put a block alongside the swing frame for a purchase block and we all got on the end of the pole. We flipped it over and over until we had it back up. We got some water and poured it in. They had some old oil to put in. We filled it, fired it up, and it ran. We hooked onto our go-devil and away we went.

We got back to Holbrook Camp about midnight. Well, my dad was some wild, wondering what had happened to us. He was just about to go out looking. He would have had to walk because his pickup, along with the pumps and other gear, had already gone out. They had been shipped on the last boat to Whitehorse in September. We didn't tell him what had happened to the cat, not till years later.

The truck came the next day and we loaded up the cat. It was eight below, Fahrenheit. There was only room for the driver and one person in those trucks, so Tony and I rode in the back. That was a long haul—60 miles over those ridges. It was hard for the driver to see the road in the whiteout conditions. Tony and I were so cold that we'd jump out on the hills and run behind to get warmed up. Eventually we got to the river. The ferry, which ran on cables with the current, was making its last trip just to get us out. There was already a lot of slush ice in the river. We got over to the other side in the dark. The ferry was pulled out the next day, and it was the last thing that ever crossed the Yukon River that fall.

A couple of days later my dad flew out on Canadian Pacific's Lodestar airplane. CP had scheduled flights between Dawson City and Whitehorse. They would fly until the temperature reached 40 below. Tony and I had decided to stay in Dawson for the winter, but my dad was headed for a job in Horsefly, pumping out a mine shaft on the old Dougherty Place. Some of those shafts had been put down many years ago. They didn't know what was in the bottom, so they were going to pump them out.

A section of the Top of the World Highway between Sixty Mile and Dawson City as it looked in October 1946. Tex and Tony were so cold in the back of the truck that they'd jump out on the hills and run to warm up.

Tony and I stayed at the Pearl Harbour Hotel for a couple of days and then moved back to our house on Fifth Avenue. The weather got colder and colder. The two-ton Holt cat had been put away in a shed there. We were told that for $900 we could buy it and two sleighs. That was our first opportunity to get into the cat business, but we only had $500 apiece to live on, so we didn't do it. As the winter went on we could see the potential for hauling wood. The town was very short of wood due to the extreme cold and the wood being so far away. It all had to be brought by horses or cats.

Tony managed to get a job with the town. He went around pulling a handsleigh with blowtorches, thawing out pipes. The town looked after its own buildings and the waterworks. I got a job with Ragnar Nelsen, hauling hay and wood. He had several

Thirty cords of wood being hauled onto the Yukon River, headed for Dawson City. The winter of 1946 recorded temperatures down to minus 83 degrees Fahrenheit, and Dawson was very short of wood.

teams of horses and sleighs. I hauled hay across the river from Sunnydale to McCormick's Transportation in Dawson. They had a big building right across Third Avenue where they kept horses, hay, cats, freight, and trucks. The weather got colder. By the end of November it was 35 below zero day after day.

The next job I did for Ragnar was to haul wood from the Arlington Roadhouse. It was up near the airport, out of Dawson. He had a woodcutter who brought the sixteen-foot lengths from the bush and dumped it there. The wood was small in diameter and had been killed in a fire, so it was quite light. I had a four-horse team and a helper. We'd load up a couple of sleighs and head out on the road, down the tailing pile and down the Klondike River. I'd come up one day, stay at the Arlington overnight, and go back the next day.

Nels Kiested owned the Arlington at that time. He'd warned me about the possibility of those horses getting frostbitten lungs from breathing the cold air. The next morning it was 40 below and old Nels said, "I think this is the morning you do it. I've got some gunny sacks here and you'd better wrap their noses up."

We did that and we made it down to Dawson that day. By God that was a cold trip!

Another job I did that winter was butchering pigs. The Sister Superior of St. Mary's Hospital couldn't find anybody to do it. I had learned how it was done from working on ranches. It was bitterly cold. I'd dip the pigs in the hot water, and by the time I got them out and started scraping the hair, ice would be forming on them.

Tony and I would go back to the house about five o'clock at night. It would often be 40 below outside and 30 below inside. We'd light the fire, but the house never really got warm. Our beds were always cold. The water never thawed out in the bucket in the kitchen. We had a big heater and a cookstove, but we couldn't keep the place warm.

One night Tony was going to peel potatoes for supper. He got some out of the sack by the back door and accidentally dropped one. It rolled all the way through the house, just like a rock, and hit the front door. Those houses were all slopes and slants from being built on the permafrost.

We didn't have much money for wood, so we decided to make a deal with Pearl at the Pearl Harbour. She said we could get a room there for $15 a month between the two of us. We could afford it, so we moved in.

On Christmas Eve it was 60 below zero, and on New Year's Eve it was 65 below. The temperature wasn't going to keep any of us from the big New Year's dance. One of the locals had a 1935 Ford, and he was determined to drive his girlfriend to the dance. He got stuck, and we were out there in our oxfords pushing him out of the snowbank. There wasn't any antifreeze in those days, so he drained the car when he got to the dance and that's where it stayed.

The winter dragged on and the wood situation got worse. The hotel burned a lot of wood. There was a basement, main floor, and two floors above that. They'd get a whole sleighload dumped on the sidewalk, and the tenants would buck it up and throw it in the basement. It kept that so-called wood furnace just a humping, as well as the woodstoves up on the main floor. There was a night watchman who kept the fires going and watched for unwanted fires. The hotel had hundreds of feet of stovepipe, much of it running laterally through the halls and then up to the next floor and finally out through the roof. Creosote dripped from the joints. It was a real firetrap. Many places did burn that winter, but the Pearl Harbour survived.

In January it got even colder. Tony's lungs got frostbitten and he began spitting up blood. He was unable to work. In February the temperature went down to 83 below by the powerhouse at the mouth of the Klondike. The government thermometer said 76 below. It stayed there for three or four days. We had to have the opening of our parkas at least six inches from our faces so that we had a kind of tunnel. That way the air warmed up a bit before we breathed it, otherwise our lungs would freeze.

We used to eat at the F and F Café, which was about three blocks from the Pearl Harbour. It was owned by a Japanese fellow by the name of Mitch. We'd hike up there, and when we opened the door, there'd be a big explosion from the humidity in the restaurant coming out and hitting that cold air. It really was a sight.

We didn't even have the sun to warm up the temperature a bit. There was five hours of dusk and the rest of the time it was dark. There were about 800 people living in town, and the smoke coming out of all of the stovepipes looked like spikes going straight up into the fog. The fog was about a hundred feet above the buildings, so it looked like we were spiked to the ground from the fogbank.

Nothing much moved. Neither the cats or the horses worked, so things were getting pretty desperate. The only communication we had with the outside world was by telegraph through the Army Signal Corps. There was a soldier working there by the name of Bill Bushell, who I got to know quite well.

Many old-timers froze to death in their cabins on the creeks and around town that winter. At the morgue there were ten men leaned up against the wall because they couldn't bury them until the ground was warmed up enough for the gravediggers to dig graves.

Then one day the weather broke, and it warmed up to twenty below zero. It felt like you could just rush outside, tear all your clothes off, and run around in the snow! It was a great relief.

Everything started to move again. The cats began hauling wood to town, and people were delivering wood with horses and sleighs. The town was very short of meat, so McCormick's Transportation organized a cat train to go to Tok Junction, Alaska, to get a load of grub, meat, and fuel. There were three 3T-D7's, a TD9, three or four sleighs, and a caboose for living quarters on the trail. I was supposed to go, but somehow or other, when the time came there wasn't room for me. I was always sorry I didn't make that trip. It was about 200 miles west, across country.

On the day they were leaving, all the cats were angle parked at the sidewalk in front of the Occidental and the New Westminster hotels. It was an odd sight. The cats were all running while the boys were in having their last drinks before they hooked up to the sleighs to leave town.

It ended up being six weeks before they got back. They had a terrible trip, with creeks overflowing and bad glaciers to cross. The TD9 broke down in California Creek, and they had to leave it there. When they went back, just the seat and hood were sticking out of the ice. It had got iced in by a glacier. They had to blow it out with dynamite, load it on a sleigh, and haul it back to Dawson.

One of the other cats broke through a creek just as it was climbing out the other side. The back end went down until it was almost vertical. The front end was out of the water and the back was in right up to the top of the fuel tank. The fuel cap wasn't under, so they were able to keep it running, but they spent many hours trying to get it out. It was the lead cat, so they wanted to get around to the front to hook on and pull it out. It was lucky that the fuel cap didn't go under or they would have had a terrible time getting the ice out of it.

One event of interest that winter in Dawson was the ringing of the Catholic Church bell every morning at eight o'clock. There were about a thousand sleigh dogs tied up in town, and the minute that church bell rang, all those dogs would howl. What a chorus!

By the time spring was coming, Tony and I got a job in a woodcamp back of the airport. We were cutting wood for an old Frenchman called Sansouci. It was

Tony at the black wood-cutting cabin behind the Dawson City airport. It was twelve feet by twelve feet, with one small window, three bunks, and a little cookstove.

some camp. There was a cabin, about twelve feet by twelve feet, with just room for three bunks, a small cookstove, and one window. It was built out of burnt logs. Sansouci had a permit to cut wood there in an old burn. We'd cut and pack the wood out to the road.

It wasn't long before everything was black: the snow, our clothes, our blankets, and our food. We had to melt snow for water, so we washed in black water. The buckskin team was black, and so were we. We didn't make much money, but it was a job and a place to stay.

When we finished up there, we went back to town. I had earned a few dollars and I had sold my radio, so I went back to the Pearl Harbour, paid my bill, and stayed on there. I was right down to bare bones for money. It was like the days in Kamloops when I was down to a cup of coffee and one piece of toast.

Then I managed to get a job with the government. They were opening up the roads around the area—Dominion, Gold Run, and Hunker. Glaciers had covered up the road through the winter, so they needed crews to go out there with picks and shovels. The mining companies were starting to thaw ground and strip where the Yukon Consolidated Mining Company dredges worked. We were able to stay in their camps, so we had a place to eat and sleep. It was a really warm spring. We worked with our shirts off, picking ice and shovelling it over the bank. I got the best suntan working on those glaciers.

One spring day, Ole Medby came to town for some grub and a little fun. He stayed for about a week. I was there the morning he left to go back to Sixty Mile. He had about seven dogs hooked up. He loaded up his sleigh at McCormick's barn and headed for the river. There was one last power pole on the riverbank a little way off to the right side of the trail. The lead dog headed for that pole. Ole yelled, "Haw! Haw!" That call means "go left." That dog was going "Gee!" He went up to the pole and lifted his leg. So did the next dog and the next and the next one. The last few dogs didn't have a chance. There were too many ahead who'd already done it, so they were dragged off past the pole and back onto the trail.

Hunker Dome Camp, Tex's home while repairing roads for the Yukon government. It had a roadhouse and cabins and was operated by Joe Fournier.

Wes Elliot thawing culverts on the roads around Dawson City with a steam boiler. It burned wood to heat water to make steam.

Tex loading gravel in the spring of 1947 to fill the mud holes in the roads. It sure warmed up!

Loading gravel through a trap at Gold Run. It sure beat loading by hand.

That summer Tony got a job with Yukon Consolidated Mining Company on a Bucyrus Erie drill. It was mounted on a track-type carrier. He drilled for them for many years. I carried on with the government, building roads and driving gravel truck.

Later in the fall, I didn't know what I was going to do. A friend of mine wanted to go "outside" in the worst way. We decided to go to Wells and work underground for Cariboo Gold Quartz. I stayed with my friend Kenny Lindquist, who had moved there from the Harper Ranch with his family.

The mine went down 1,500 feet under Jack-o'-Clubs Lake. The deepest that I went down was 600 feet. We had to buy "bone-dry" clothes and rubber boots. They gave us a hard hat with an electric light. We packed a big battery on our backs to power it.

Just before we started our shift underground, we went into the aluminum room. Everyone sat in this big room and aluminum dust was pumped into it. We sat there and breathed that for five or ten minutes. The idea was to coat our lungs to protect them from silicosis. Today, people are horrified to hear of it.

When we left the aluminum room, we picked up our lights and batteries, which had been recharged, put them on, and met our shifter. We got into the mine cars with all the other men, and the train took us through the portal, which is the entrance. We went way back into the mountain. I was wondering where I was going and if the train would ever stop. Eventually it did and some of the fellows got off here and then some there. Finally I got off with the shifter. There were electric lights in the top of the main tunnel where the train ran, so we could see a bit in there. We got into a cage that took us down two or three levels. Then we walked through the dark with only our headlamps on. There was just my shifter and me, slopping through the water dripping constantly from the ceiling. We'd hear the odd bit of rotten rock falling into the water.

We walked and walked and then got into a skip, a small box that took us to another level in the mine. We got out and walked some more. Finally we came around a corner and saw this huge cavern. There was about six inches of water and a big pile of muck in it. A little ore car and a rusty old shovel sat in the water. My shifter said, "This is where you're going to work. You'll load that car and then push it up out of here and down this tunnel."

He took me back and showed me where there was a big hole in the side of the tunnel. It was covered with steel bars and that's where I was to dump the car. It was called a grizzly. All the fine stuff went through, and the bigger pieces had to be broken up with a sledgehammer so they would go between the bars. He said, "I'll be back to get you because you'll never find your way out."

I loaded up the car, but I could not move it. I felt down in the water around the wheels. The back two wheels were off the track. Of course I couldn't lift it, so I had to shovel it out until I could. Then I loaded it up again, pushed it down to the grizzly, dumped it, and broke up the big rocks. I felt like I was in Alcatraz, using that big sledgehammer. I wondered where I'd gone wrong in life.

My light fell off my hat while I was unloading the car. It went out, leaving me in total blackness. I had been in some black places in my life but nothing like that. The only sound was the drip, drip, drip of the water from the ceiling. I was very anxious to get that light hooked back up again. I did, but then I started to wonder if the shifter would ever come back. Finally he came and led me out of there. After a few days I got to know my way and I'd go in by myself and work all day.

At night I'd go up to the main tunnel and meet the train. There might be 50 or 60 men walking along. Everybody was smoking and they were all sweating. The steam rose from their bodies. It was eerie. The steam created a kind of fog over all the men as they walked along, one behind the other in that ghostly light.

Suddenly I heard a great big "whoomph" and felt something hit me in the back, pushing me forward and then backing off. Smoke and steam shot ahead about ten feet, stopped, and backed up. I learned later that at quitting time the miners set off their blasts all through the mountain. The concussion works its way through the tunnels up to the open air above. We would feel the force of it against our backs.

I worked at that job for about a month and a half until one day I woke up as sick as a dog. I had chicken pox.

5

Something Fishy
(1947-1951)

When I started recuperating, I couldn't go to work right away, so I decided to jump on a bus and go to Williams Lake to visit some of my friends. I went into the old Lakeview Hotel, and the first person I met was Bert Roberts. He asked, "What are you doing now?"

I told him that I'd been driving truck and running cat in the Yukon since I quit cowboying in the Chilcotin.

He said, "I've got a truck working for the International Pacific Salmon Commission out at Farwell Canyon. They're building six fish ladders there. The truck is broke down, but it'll be running again in a few days. You could come and run it if you like. I'll pay you a dollar an hour."

I said, "Sure."

I couldn't believe that Bert would pay me a dollar an hour to drive a truck! He took me down to a real nice camp at Farwell and introduced me to Hughie Dunlop, who would be my boss. Hughie's wife Eva did the cooking. There were about ten or twelve men there. I felt well enough to drive truck, and I thought maybe I'd just stay down here. I phoned up the Lindquists and told them that I wasn't going to be back for awhile.

The truck had been left parked in a hazardous spot above the fish ladders. I went over that night to have a look at it. It was on a real narrow trail on the edge of the boiling Chilcotin River.

Fish ladders were under construction in Farwell Canyon on the Chilcotin River in the fall of 1947. The camp of the International Pacific Salmon Fisheries Commission is down near the river in the background.

The sector gear was gone in the steering, so we had to wait for the parts to come. While I was waiting, I loaded trucks with sand and gravel by shovel. I didn't mind working. There were two guys on one side and myself on the other, and I could load as fast as they could together. The boss seemed to notice. He was really good to me, and I sure liked him.

One day Hughie said, "Well, that damn truck is not ready yet, but I've got this little jeep here. Twice a week we use it to go to town to pick up parts and laundry and grub. Maybe you'd like to do that."

"Sure," I said.

I did that for awhile, every so often thinking about that truck. Finally the parts came for it. The mechanic put them in and then it was ready for me to move. I'll never forget how all the fellows working on the fish ladders on the other side of the river stopped and looked as I walked over to the truck. They didn't know if I could drive that truck out of there or not. There was only about a foot between the back wheel and the very edge of the trail. Then it was straight down, 60 feet to the river. It was a matter of backing it out to one switchback and then driving it forward up the next one and backing it up the next, sort of seesawing up the face of the rock. The river was on my side of the truck, so if it went over, I'd never get a chance to jump out.

I was a little scared because I'd never driven that type of truck before. I wasn't sure what the ratio of the rear-end was or if it was a smooth accelerator. It was also a cab-over, and I hadn't ever driven one of them.

Everyone was watching me as I got into the cab and started the engine. I put it in reverse and slowly backed along

Two of Tex's friends who worked for the Salmon Commission at Farwell Canyon. They were out hunting deer in the fall.

to the first corner. I shifted into first and drove up the next pitch. Then I pulled out onto the edge and backed up the next one and I was home free.

After that nobody ever questioned my driving ability. I guess I was in with that outfit. I stayed with them for four years, doing work for the International Pacific Salmon Commission, which was a government outfit, run by the U.S. and Canadian governments since 1937. It was fixing up salmon habitat in the Pacific Northwest, constructing fish ladders and hatcheries in the area.

The company had bought a new TD9 cat down at Galbraith's in Vernon and had it hauled up the week before Christmas of 1947. They'd also brought an operator for it. He was going to work on the road—a terrible road from Riske Creek to Farwell. I told Hughie that I'd run cat in the Yukon.

He said, "If this guy doesn't come back after Christmas, you can run that cat."

I was sure hoping that he wouldn't come back.

I arrived back in Williams Lake after the Christmas holidays, just after New Year's. I met Hughie and his wife and got a ride with them to Riske Creek. Hughie told me that the fellow wasn't coming back and the cat job was mine. Boy, was I happy to hear that.

The one problem was that I never had told Hughie that although I'd run a cat, I hadn't run one with a blade on it. I was going to be just ploughing snow at first, so I figured that by the time I had to move dirt I'd be okay. I ploughed snow all the way down to Farwell and got the camp opened up. The rest of the winter I ploughed back and forth to Riske Creek, right up to the main road at Bert Roberts' store.

God, the wind blew and blew. It got colder and colder. It went down to 25 below and the snow drifted terribly. I couldn't keep up to it. Finally Doug Hembrough, the mechanic, went on with me. We double-shifted that cat for a couple of weeks trying to keep the road open. We'd have to make traps off to the side to try to catch the drifts before they got onto the road. We had great big ditches full, and the snow was packed in so tight that we could walk on it with the cat. We chipped it out in huge chunks all winter long.

Spring came and the company hired more men to work on the fish ladders again. They needed cat work done down there. The first bit of dirt I had to move for Hughie was on a piece of road just up from the ladders on our main road. It had all sloughed in from the spring thaw, and the loose gravel had pretty well filled in the whole road. He wanted it all dug out and widened.

It was a Friday when I started. Hughie had gone home about two o'clock that day. He and Eva lived in a cabin at Bert Roberts' place. I dug into that gravel and widened it out, but when it came to doing the finishing, I just could not get it smooth. I was laying these terrible humps. I had managed to operate the blade well enough through the winter because the ground was frozen. When the blade hit the frozen dirt under the snow, it would just slide along, so it always looked great. But I could not get onto using the blade on that ground. If I put it down I'd dig a hole, and

*Now what? Tex looking at the Salmon
Commission's cat, bogged down near Riske Creek.*

if I lifted it up I'd have a hump. So I had a hump and a hole and a hump and a hole. I back-bladed it this way and that way. Finally I gave up and left it.

I was back up there again early Monday morning, anxious to get it fixed before Hughie arrived. I'd just started the cat up when he came sailing along. He had a 1939 Dodge sedan. He came rolling around the corner and down onto that piece of road. When he hit those humps, the hood flew right off his car. Well, was he ever upset. He walked all over me. I couldn't say a word. He had finally found out that I was not a blade-man.

I expected to be fired right there, but he put the hood back on his car and said, "You'd better get that straightened out."

I guess Hughie had confidence in me, because there were some pretty precarious places down along the river where we put in the fish ladders. I was working along the solid rock with the blasting going on ahead. We didn't make the road very wide.

Delmer Jasper with the Salmon Commission's TD9 cat on the truck. Delmer, Tex, and George McNaughton were moving it to Horsefly from Farwell Canyon in 1948.

We only needed access along the riverbank a short way beyond where the fish ladders were being installed. There were a lot of exciting moments since there were, at most, only inches in which to manoeuvre. I figured that if I slipped off the rock and into the river, I'd be able to swim, as long as I didn't get hung up on the cat. Fortunately I didn't slide off.

When we finished there we headed out to Horsefly Lake, where the salmon hatchery was going to be built. The Salmon Commission's truck wasn't available to haul the cat, so they suggested that I walk it from Farwell Canyon to Riske Creek. When I got to Riske Creek the truck still wasn't there, so I walked it to Williams Lake. That was a long old hike: 40 miles, bouncing over the rocks on a TD9. It was worse than riding a razor-backed horse, which I'd done on that road once before. I was sure happy that the truck was available for the rest of the trip.

The truck driver was George McNaughton, and he, Delmer Jasper, and I loaded the cat and hauled it to Horsefly. I started building a road to the Little Horsefly River. It bordered on the Red Jacket Lodge property, which was owned by the Hubbards. I'd been working on the road for a few days when I happened to look into the bush and saw Mrs. Hubbard. She was waving a big butcher knife and yelling, "University Bastard! Stop!"

So I did. The engineer came along shortly and I told him what had happened. He said he'd get some of the crew to see that I wasn't attacked or shot at. On the fourth day we were nearing the bridge site when we saw a big tent some distance ahead. I walked up and saw a note on the side of it. It said PRIVATE PROPERTY. The engineer came along, looked at it, and said, "If it's still there when you get to it with the cat, just push it off the right-of-way."

By the time I'd cleared the road up to that point, it had been taken down. We learned later that those people were quite eccentric, to the point where they might have caused harm to the crew.

There was terrible flooding in the spring of 1948. Access to the fish ladders was difficult in places like Hell's Gate and Farwell Canyon, and it was really critical at Lillooet, so the engineer said, "You'd better take the big truck and the cat down there and rebuild the road to the fish ladders at the mouth of Bridge River."

I took my old dog, Jack, and some clean clothes and away I went. I drove down to Kelly Lake, up over Pavilion Mountain, and on to Lillooet. The road was steep and narrow. I was enjoying the trip but it was hotter than blazes. There weren't any culverts in those days, so the water just ran across the road. I stopped at these little streams to get a nice cold drink. I noticed that Jack was suffering from the heat, so I put him up on the seat of the cat. It was cooler than riding in the cab of the truck.

We arrived in Lillooet. I was told that the hotel was at the far end of Main Street. I drove slowly along, saw a wide spot, and pulled the truck over and parked. I jumped out and looked up at the cat. There were wires hanging all over the canopy and trailing down both sides of the truck and all the way down the street.

All of a sudden I saw a police car, lights flashing and siren wailing, racing toward me. It was zigzagging through all that destruction. The policeman jumped out of his car and ran up to me. He asked me what the hell I thought I was doing, who was I, where did I come from, and did I have a driver's licence? He took a quick breath and continued, what was I going to do about this mess? All the people in Lillooet were going to be electrocuted if I didn't do something right away and on and on.

I was threading my belt back through the loops of my pants. The sweat had been running down my back all afternoon and I'd taken it off.

He said, "When you're talking to me keep your hands out of your pockets."

"My hands aren't in my pockets," I replied, "and I haven't even had a chance to say a word."

Just then I noticed Jack kind of crouching and heading for the police car. There was a big black lab in it, and the window was open. Well, my dog leaped in through that window and soon there was the biggest dogfight you ever saw going on inside that car. The policeman went wild. "You get that dog out of there and off my dog," he yelled. "He's killing my dog. I'll put you in jail for this!"

I opened the door, grabbed Jack by the tail, and pulled them both out onto the ground. They wouldn't let go of each other. Finally the policeman got his dog by the tail and we pulled them apart. He got his back into his car, all covered in blood, and drove away. Jack didn't have any marks on him, not from that fight anyway.

I was looking around and wondering what to do next. I looked up the street and saw some fellows with a truck and some ladders, hooking up the wires. I went up and talked to them. They were real nice about it. They said they'd have it all fixed in an hour or

*The Salmon Commission was building the fish hatchery at
Horsefly Lake in 1948. The lumber came from Gardener's mill
at Horsefly Lake, and the cement and steel were shipped up
from Vancouver on the Pacific Great Eastern Railway.*

so. They put the wires up a little higher, so I was able to drive
out of town the next morning to Bridge River.

I worked there for two weeks and enjoyed it. One of the
company's engineers came up from Vancouver, approved the job,
and said I could go back to Horsefly.

I put in the rest of that summer and fall building the road to
the Little Horsefly River. The rest of the crew were working on
the new bridge. The company also wanted to get some of the
camp buildings done before winter, so there was a lot of activity.

One day late in the fall there wasn't any work for the cat.
The boss said, "Take the dump truck and go to Williams Lake
for a load of cement. The truck has been broken down and there's
a load of gravel in the box, so you'll have to empty that out."

The mechanic said the truck was ready to go, so I fired it up.
It sounded like the muffler was off. I raised the box to fix it. The
gravel was frozen into the box, so I figured I'd have to use some

Building the bridge across the Little Horsefly River.

heat later to thaw it. We'd usually light a woodfire on top of the gravel to loosen it up.

I leaned over the frame and tried to jam the muffler back onto the exhaust pipe. It was making a lot of noise. Then I felt something on my back. I thought it was one of the boys and looked around. The box was coming down! I pulled my arm back and slid myself toward the cab. I got out, but not before it caught my hat and a bunch of my hair between the box and the frame.

The lumber for the job came from Gardener's mill on Horsefly Lake, and the steel and cement were shipped up from Vancouver. It came by train to Williams Lake and was hauled out by truck. While the camp was being built, the crew stayed at the lodge at Horsefly Landing. It was a lively place on weekends. We had a lot of great times.

I met Marj Kennedy during one of those weekends that summer of 1948. She was cooking for the Hume and Rumble Pole Company farther up Horsefly Lake, and she came down on weekends. We met at a dance at Horsefly and started going together.

Around Christmastime we decided to get married. We went down to my dad's place in Lumby. By this time he and my mother weren't together anymore. He'd bought 40 acres of land with some good placer claims on it. My brother Tony was down from

*Tex, Marj Kennedy, Bob Fosbery, and Betty and Tony Fosbery
at Bob's home at Lumby. They were on their way to Vancouver
where Tex and Marj were married in 1948.*

the Yukon that Christmas, so we all drove to Vancouver. Marj
and I were married in the old Anglican church at the corner of
Georgia and Burrard streets.

We came back to Horsefly and moved into a house at the
hatchery site, where I continued working until just before
Christmas 1949. The company had brought in another cat from
Vancouver, so between the two of us we had all the ponds built
and the landscaping done around the buildings.

They told me that I'd be going down to work at Hell's Gate
for the winter. Marj and I stayed at her mother's place at Horsefly
for Christmas and then headed out. I had a 1946 Chev car that
I'd bought from Art Evans at Williams Lake Motors. We packed
it up with a few dynamite boxes filled with supplies, along with
some blankets and Jack. It was bitterly cold the day we left.

We got down to the church at the Indian Reserve just north of Cache Creek and hit a terrible blizzard and big snowdrifts. I slid off the road and had one hell of a time shovelling my way out. We finally got to Cache Creek and gassed up the car. There wasn't much at Cache Creek in those days. By the time we got to Spences Bridge, it was dark. The hotel clerk asked, "How far are you going?"

"Hell's Gate," I replied.

"No. The canyon is closed as far as Lytton," he said. "But there'll be a D7 cat coming along from Merritt in a day or so to plough it out."

We sat in that old barn of a hotel for two days. We didn't have much money, so I was sure hoping that cat would come along soon. It did, and as it rattled on by the hotel, we jumped in our car and followed it. What a long trek that was, at three miles an hour all the way to Lytton. That was as far as the cat was going, even though the road was still closed beyond there.

It was New Year's Eve. We got a room at the motel in Lytton. The next day I decided that I'd better send Marj back to Horsefly. I put her on the train to Ashcroft, where she caught the bus to Williams Lake. Then she got a ride with George Niquidet, who operated a stage line between there and Horsefly.

"It was 50 degrees below zero when we got to Horsefly," she told me later. She had to walk two or three miles to her mother's place. She had a terrible time because there were so many moose on the road. They didn't want to go off into the deep snow and they didn't want to be driven along. She finally made it through, but it was a pretty bad experience for her.

While I was in Lytton I found out that one of the problems with the road was near Alexandra Lodge. The highway construction company had made a big blast just after Christmas and then shut down until New Year's. It had started snowing so much that they couldn't carry on until it quit.

I had to get to work. I was supposed to be at Hell's Gate on January 2. I made arrangements to leave my car at Lytton. I took Jack and some personal gear and caught the train that night. The conductor said, "We're not stopping at Hell's Gate. We're not stopping just to let you off. The snowslide situation makes it too dangerous. The best I can do is slow down the train and you'll have to jump."

He stood out between the two cars with me, and he pulled the cord to signal the engineer when we neared Hell's Gate. The train slowed. "When I tell you to jump, you jump," he said.

We peered out into the darkness. It was still snowing. We couldn't see anything. Then all of a sudden there were some black objects down in the snow, about 50 feet below the tracks. He yelled, "There it is! There it is! Jump!"

I jumped. I had my dog under one arm and my duffel bag under the other arm. I went right down to my neck in snow. Jack started struggling to get free. I could hear the train picking up speed and soon it was rattling away into the darkness. It became deathly quiet as I stood there in the snow.

I managed to wallow over to the edge of the snowdrift and rolled and crawled down toward the buildings. It was so dark. I didn't even know if there was anybody there. I just kept on knocking on doors. Eventually I came to a bunkhouse. A fellow came to the door. I was sure glad to see him. It turned out to be Bob Rennie, the man in charge of the job. I was in a nice warm place at last.

I was pretty happy the next day to be working again. I also got a chance to look at my surroundings. It was about 700 feet from the river up to the highway. There was a trail that the men used to get to work, or else they came by train, which was partway up to the highway. That trail up the mountain looked almost hopeless right then. There was so much snow, and it was still snowing.

On the weekend I told Bob that I'd like to move my wife from Horsefly down to the motel at The Tunnels. On Sunday morning Jack and I walked along the railway track about five miles up past China Bar. I got onto the highway and walked five miles back to The Tunnels. I spoke to the proprietors of the motel, an older couple by the name of Thompson, and said, "I'd like to rent a cabin for the winter. As soon as the road opens up I'll be moving my wife down from the Cariboo."

"That's no problem," he replied. "But we don't have any wood. You'll have to cut your own."

With those arrangements made I walked back along the highway to where the trail went down over the edge of the mountain. There was a garage there where some of the men left their cars. I found where the trail was supposed to be and broke it open the best I could down to Hell's Gate. The next week the road was opened up as far as the slide. They were going to start working on it again.

I phoned Marj. She came down with her brother, Murray, who was also going to be working at Hell's Gate for the winter. They came down by train to Lytton. It was Saturday, so I went up on the way-freight and met them. I got my car, and we went to the grocery store. The road foreman came in and asked, "Where are you headed?"

"Hell's Gate," I replied.

"Well I suggest that you get enough grub for at least two weeks," he said. "I don't know if they'll be able to work on the road or not."

When we arrived at the motel the snowbanks were so high that I couldn't get the car off the road. I dug a trail through the snowbank and we packed our grub to the cabin. Throughout the weekend I kept digging away until I got the car off the road. It was the last vehicle down that road until April.

The cabin we rented was meant strictly for summer living. It was very small, and the walls were only one thickness of lumber with some wallpaper on them. There was cold running water that came from up the mountain. We had an inside bathroom, which was quite a luxury, but we only had a small airtight heater for cooking. The wood had to be cut very short to fit in that stove, and it was hard to keep a fire going at night. It went down to 25 degrees below, so it got damned cold in that shack.

We weren't able to work on the fish ladders because of all the snow, but we worked in the shop. There was a D4 cat down there that I was supposed to run. Someone had left water in it over the Christmas holidays, so it had a broken block. We used an Army jeep and a block and tackle to drag it into the shop. We put a patch on the block and fixed the starting motor.

It was a long and tough winter, continually snowing. We shovelled narrow trails between the bunkhouse, cookhouse, powerhouse, and shop. They looked like tunnels of snow. We threw the snow up as high as we could, and by the time spring came there was nine feet of snow on the level. There were 200 cats working for the CPR between Hope and Jasper trying to keep the railroad open. They did a pretty good job as I remember.

My car just disappeared. In the spring I noticed something shiny sticking out of the snow. It was the antenna. I'd been walking over the top of my car all winter. Marj found a car that winter, too. She was sawing wood when the Swede-saw hit something. She cleaned the snow away. It was a car that someone had abandoned.

Every second Friday night I stayed in camp, and in the morning I'd catch the way-freight to North Bend to buy groceries for us and for the Thompsons. Then I'd catch the next way-freight back to Hell's Gate. I would try to arrange my pack so that I could take everything in one trip up to the highway. It wasn't easy to walk along the snowslides with this big load on my shoulders, trying not to slip off the retaining walls.

There were a lot of deer killed in snowslides that winter. I almost got it myself one Monday morning while trying to get down to camp. It had snowed all weekend, and I was more or less swimming straight down through the deep snow. Suddenly the whole thing started to move. It sucked me down so that only my head was sticking out. Poor old Jack was behind me somewhere. He always travelled up and down with me. I got my arms freed up and managed to get my big coat off. I put it under my knees on the downhill side and worked my way out. Then I got Jack out. I gave up for the day and went back home.

The next day I tried a different place, but I couldn't get down. The third day I went on the original trail and met some of the boys coming up from camp. They were looking for me.

I had another close call later that winter. I used to walk through two tunnels on the highway on my way to work. They were about a hundred yards apart. One morning I was almost halfway between them when I heard a whispering noise up on the mountain. I looked up and saw a huge snowslide. I turned and ran back toward the tunnel. I just made it in when there was a loud rumbling and everything disappeared in the biggest whiteout you could imagine. I couldn't see anything for several minutes. I hoped I wasn't trapped. Finally I saw a tiny hole near the top of the tunnel. I crawled up, scraped away some snow, and managed to crawl out. That was a close one.

That slide had gone right down to the railroad track. It was really smooth, so I got the idea of using it as a shortcut to work. I'd go inside the tunnel, crawl up through the hole, get on my snowshovel, and go ripping down the 700 feet to the track. I used my heels for braking. Then I'd walk along the track for a mile and a half to the bridge that crossed over to the other side of Hell's Gate.

One morning I was walking along and had just about reached the bridge. There was a steam engine on the track with a rotary snowplough on the front and a caboose on the back. The railroaders were patrolling the track, blowing off snowslides. I didn't see anybody in the caboose as I walked up to it. I walked by the engine and there was nobody up in the cab. Then I looked at the snowplough and there was a fellow inside that great big thing tightening bolts.

The rotary had big steel paddles on the front of it. When it was wound up, the centrifugal force would cause the paddles to swing out, catch the snow, and force it out through a big pipe, blowing it onto the river.

"Where is everybody?" I asked the man in the plough. "Where's the head brakeman and the engineer and the fireman?"

"Oh, they're up in the section house having coffee," he said.

We talked for a few minutes and I carried on toward the bridge. I was about halfway across, with the river roaring underneath and the wind blowing all around me, when I heard another sound. I turned and saw the biggest snowslide. It took the engine, the fellow, the plough, and the caboose right off the track, over the bank, and down 60 feet into the river. All that was sticking out was one corner of the engine.

That was a terrible tragedy. I couldn't help thinking that if I had stayed talking for a few more minutes I'd have been with that fellow in the river. In the spring they found his body near Hope. There were four men, three from the section crews, killed in that area by snowslides that winter.

I was certainly glad to see spring come. Marj hadn't been out of there since January 15, so she was getting bushed. At Easter, since it was a long weekend, we decided to walk down to Alexandra Lodge for a change. It was about four miles south on the highway, which had cleared off enough so we could walk quite easily. We arrived at the lodge and be darned if they didn't have ice cream. So we had ice cream and a cup of tea and walked back home. It was the highlight of that weekend.

One day in the early spring, old Mr. Thompson said he'd seen a bear nearby, sitting under a tree. We hadn't had any fresh meat all winter, so I went out and found him. I shot him with a .22, dragged him home, and pulled the hide off. We tried to eat

*Tex worked on the construction of the fish
ladder at Hell's Gate in 1950 and 1951.*

him, but he was so tough. Finally we boiled it, and that softened it up enough to eat. Everybody was happy to have a change of diet from wieners and bully beef.

A few days later I looked up from the job and saw a cat coming along from Boston Bar, making a trail on the highway. That was the start of it. They opened up the road and the construction crew got back to work.

We stayed at that job all that summer and the next winter. I walked every day up and down the trail, so I got to be in pretty good shape.

The next Easter we drove up to Marj's mother's place at Horsefly. It was spring break-up, and we got stuck in the mud on the Horsefly Road near China Cabin. We spent the rest of the night in the car. George Niquidet came along about four in the morning. He was travelling on the frost, going to Williams Lake for freight. He pulled us out, and we carried on to Marj's mother's home, where we stayed for nearly a week.

It turned really cold for our trip back to Hell's Gate. We arrived in the middle of the night, unlocked the door, and tried to push it open. It would spring open at the top but not at the bottom. I went around the cabin, opened the bedroom window, and stepped inside over the window sill. I expected there to be a drop to the floor, but I only stepped down a little way before I was standing on it. What was going on? I couldn't imagine.

I got the flashlight and shone it inside. There was about a foot of ice on top of the floor! We had left the water running a bit so it wouldn't freeze. The drain had frozen and the water then spilled out onto the floor. It had been freezing at night and not warming up much in the daytime, so the ice was all over the cabin, right up to the draft on the stove. It was almost up to the mattress on the bed. The sink looked like Niagara Falls. We managed to make a fire and went to bed, but it was a cold night. The next day we got the axe and chopped and shovelled out the ice. It was a big job.

6

Skinning Cats in Terrace and the Yukon (1951-1954)

Later in that spring of 1951 we got a letter from Marj's brother Allen, who was working in Prince Rupert with Ray Webster. He said there was lots of work and if we ever had holidays we should come up for a visit.

As it turned out, the International Pacific Salmon Commission's fiscal year end was on March 31. The engineer said they had to wait about ten days for their new budget before continuing on with the job. I talked it over with Marj and we decided to go to Prince Rupert.

In Williams Lake I ran into the agent for Austin-Healy. He had some nice little pickups for sale. He'd give me a pretty good price and a good trade-in for my 1946 Chev. We made a deal and then set off for Prince George in our new pickup with our camping gear in the back.

We were told that the road was really bad between Prince George and Vanderhoof. We went as far as Mud River and camped there for the night. In the morning we went along a few miles over a road that was corduroyed and planked in places so we could get through the mud. We managed to stay on top of all this stuff and keep going until we came up to a fellow who was stuck down between the corduroy. He was having a lot of trouble trying to move. We helped him out, and then he came back and helped me fix it up so that I could get across.

We went along pretty well from there and finally arrived in Vanderhoof. I gassed up the pickup and reached for my wallet. No wallet. Holy lightning! All the money we had was in that wallet. We couldn't go any farther without it. I told the fellow that I'd lost my wallet and would have to go back and look for it. I don't know if he believed me or not.

We went back over that terrible road. I was sure it would be where I'd helped that fellow through the corduroy. We hunted around there and couldn't find it. We decided that it must be back where we camped. We drove all the way back to Mud River and looked around our campsite. The wallet wasn't there. I asked myself, "Now, where could it be?"

Then I remembered that I'd gone down to the creek to brush my teeth. I hurried down and sure enough, there it was, right on the edge of the water. It had slipped out of my pocket while I bent over. I was certainly happy to have it back. There was $150 in it, and that was all the money we had.

We went back to Vanderhoof, got more gas, and continued on to Decker Lake, where we camped for the night. The next day we got as far as Hazelton. Then we drove the rest of the way down the Skeena River to Terrace.

I remember counting the bridges between Hazelton and Terrace. There were 68 of them crossing little streams that ran down into the Skeena River. The road was narrow and winding. We were so glad to get to Terrace. It was warm and beautiful, with snow-covered mountains. It looked like a wonderful part of the world.

Allen and Ray had since moved from Prince Rupert to Terrace. They had a contract with Little, Houghlund, and Kerr to cut and peel poles. There were lots of good cedar poles in that area, so they were doing pretty well.

We camped out of town at a bridge on an old logging road. Then we started to look around the country. Everything was booming. Columbia Cellulose Pulp and Paper, owned by New

York people, had just moved into the area. They had picked up a tree farm licence that included the timber all the way up the Kalum Valley and Copper River and down the Skeena River. They had years and years of logging lined up. The saw logs would be shipped by train to Prince Rupert, made into Davis rafts, and towed to Vancouver. They were also building a big pulp mill in Prince Rupert.

I went to see the manager of Columbia Cellulose. I asked him if he thought it would be a good idea to move up and what were the possibilities of getting a job. I told him I was a cat operator. He said, "There'll be no problem getting a job. We'll be buying a bunch of cats somewhere down the road. You could probably work on one of those. We'll be here for 75 years. There are other things happening, too. We have a contractor here from Port McNeil with a bunch of big shovels. They're going to be building roads this summer for us. They'll have a couple of cats spreading gravel on those roads."

It sounded good, and Marj and I liked the area. The sun was shining and the mountains and the river were so beautiful. The population of Terrace was about 4,000 at that time. I said, "Let's go back. I'll quit my job and we'll pick up the little bit of stuff that we have there."

We drove to Hell's Gate and I spoke to my boss. He said, "You can go to work anytime."

I said, "No, I've changed my mind. I'm going up to Terrace to work."

I had been with them for four years, so it was time for a change. We drove back to Terrace, camping out along the way, just as we'd done on the way up and down. We were tired of camping out, so when we got to Terrace we decided to stay in a motel just outside of town. The proprietor looked at my pickup and said, "Gee, I sure like that little truck. You don't want to sell it do you?"

"Not really," I replied.

"I've got a good Model A here," he said. "I'll trade you and give you $800 to boot."

I thought it sounded like a pretty good deal. We'd have wheels *and* money. I said, "Yeah, I'll go for that."

We completed the deal the next day. Then we went to the real estate office and bought a house. It wasn't much of a house but it was a roof over our heads. It had a well and even electricity. It had an outhouse, but that was okay. It was only a half mile off the main street. It cost $2,500, but we only had to put a hundred down and had three years to pay it off.

So inside of a week I had a job, a house on an acre of land, and a car. That was the best thing that ever happened to me, and it happened so quickly.

I was working for Columbia Construction. They didn't have an opening for a cat operator right away, so I was oiling on one of the big road-building shovels. It was a Model 6 Northwest.

I couldn't get over all the activity. We had to be up on Main Street at four o'clock in the morning to catch the crummy that took us to work. I was working on the main road, but the company was also building branch roads. There were cats and gravel trucks working, and fallers falling the trees from the right-of-ways. There were even trucks hauling logs down the branch roads. The main road was only about five miles long, but it was filled with crummys, pickups, gravel trucks, and people. It was exciting. I'd never seen anything like it before.

I hadn't been around those big shovels before, either. It was quite a dirty job. I had to grease it and set tongs on the pads. The ground they were digging was rather soft. The shovels were very heavy, so they had five pads to sit on. They were twenty feet long and five feet wide. They were made of ten-by-ten timbers bolted together, with a cablestrap through each end. When it was digging, the shovel would sit on four pads and the fifth would be free behind it. I'd hook the hook into the strap on the back pad whenever he wanted to move. He would then swing the bucket with the pad attached around in front of him and lay it down in front of the other four pads. Then he'd move ahead five feet and start digging again. There were powdermen up ahead blowing the stumps, and a culvert crew behind building log culverts.

One day they told me that they'd be double-shifting one of the cats and that I could run it if I wanted the job. I was soon spreading gravel with a TD14 for 22 trucks. It sure kept me busy, staying ahead of those guys and making the roadbed fit to drive on. It was very soft. I had to take care to keep it wide and stable enough so they could back up and dump their loads over the end. I also had to make turnouts so they could pass each other. A lot of the fellows had never driven truck before and they'd dump their load in the wrong place or back over the side. Then I'd have to pull them out.

It kept me busy, but I enjoyed it. I was working ten hours a day, six days a week. My wages were a dollar and a half an hour, which was much better than the dollar an hour I'd been getting at Hell's Gate.

I worked there all summer. We had 68 days without a cloud in the sky. It was absolutely beautiful. I always say that the sun shone until the end of September, then the sky clouded up, it started to rain, and never stopped for 21 years.

In the fall, construction shut down and it was hard to find a job. I drove a dump truck for awhile and did odd jobs. We had enough money to make the house payments but hardly any for Christmas.

Ray Webster's parents had moved up from Horsefly that fall. They didn't have much money either, so they moved into our big old house with us. It was great. In January 1952 they found an old cabin on Legate Creek, about 30 miles from Terrace. They moved out there, cut some firewood, and shot a moose. It wasn't easy, but they managed well enough.

I was desperately looking for work. I wound up washing dishes in an old folks' home. I only did it for about a week. I had my name in with Columbia Cellulose, and they finally called to ask me to set chokers behind a D6 cat at one of their logging operations. There was almost five feet of snow. It was harder than washing dishes, but I was happier out there.

A few days later they asked me to walk a TD18 from Terrace to Shames, which was about 25 miles. There were no lowbeds in those days, and there was no pavement on the roads, so equipment was walked to the job sites.

My cat had an angle blade, so I was hired to build winter truck roads on some of the islands on the Skeena River. Columbia Cellulose had tried to float logs down the river and had lost them, causing big log jams. I was able to push roads to them, since the river is low in the winter. Then the heel-booms would pick the logs out of the debris and load them onto trucks, which had to have access to Highway 16. The trucks carried the logs to the railroad, where they were shipped to Watson Island at Prince Rupert.

As a blade operator, I was getting twenty cents more an hour than the fellows on the skid cats. They didn't like that.

It was the International Woodworkers of America (IWA) negotiation year. I didn't belong to the union, but I had to join. We had a strike vote, and there were only two of us who voted against a strike. That's when I started to learn about unions and how they think everybody should make the same wage. They went on strike.

I had obligations and couldn't afford to lie around, so I got in touch with Tony in the Yukon. He was working for Harold Schmidt, who was mining out at Sixty Mile. He sent word back to me that I could probably get a job up there running a D8.

Within a few days I was on the train to Prince George, where I caught a DC3 to Whitehorse and a Lodestar to Dawson City. Tony picked me up and took me out to Sixty Mile, where I went to work immediately. I made five dollars for a ten-hour day.

Using a D8 cat, I stripped the moss and overburden off the permafrost in areas where a creek ran through. These creeks were found in narrow little valleys called pups, and that's where the gold was usually found. I had to remove about seven feet of frozen black muck from on top of the gravel containing the pay. I'd start upstream and strip off the grass and brush, pushing it up the hillsides. I'd work my way down on both sides of the pup to the bottom, maybe a quarter of a mile. It took about a week. During that time, under 24 hours of sunshine, the black muck would thaw about a foot down. Then I'd go back up to where I started and push the thawed muck off, working my way down the pup again. This process continued until I was down to the gravel.

Meanwhile I'd arranged for Marj to move up. She came with Ray and Murray Webster, who were looking for work because of the strike down south.

One day when I was pushing grass and brush, I noticed two sticks poking straight up through the moss. They were about a foot high and were rounded on the ends. I got off the cat and looked at them. They were sticking out of a little bit of clear ice, and I could see that they were the ends of a ladder sticking out of a shaft. I kicked back the grass and moss and saw a big hole, about three feet by three feet. It was filled with clear blue ice, and the ladder was standing in it. That shaft had probably been there since the turn of the century.

I didn't want to disturb it, so I kept working around it. Every day or so another rung would show up until there were about twelve rungs sticking out of the ground. From a distance it looked as if there was nothing holding it up. Eventually I got to where I could see the bottom rung down in the shaft. Then I could see that the blue ice ran off upstream and downstream. There was only a foot of blue ice left before bedrock. That's where the old miners had drifted and cleaned up the gold on the bottom of the drifts. They had packed it out, put it in a bucket, wound it up to the top of the shaft, and washed out their dumps.

It was strange when all the ice was gone. I could see the remnants of a fire and smell the wet burnt wood even after all

Placer mining for Harold Schmidt at Sixty Mile in the Yukon in 1952.
Tony was pushing into the sluice and Tex was piling the tailings.

those years it was buried in the ice. I found a pick with carbide tips that were as sharp as a razor, but the rest of the iron was almost eaten away. It was just a thin shell. The piece around the handle was still there, and the handle itself was like petrified wood. I kept it on the cat for quite awhile, but eventually it got lost. I was sure sorry to lose it.

Later on, when we actually started mining, Tony was putting in the cuts and pushing them into the sluice boxes. I was pushing tailings. Four of us were double-shifting. We worked twelve hours a day, seven days a week, for two weeks, and then ten hours a day for two weeks. It was a big break when the ten-hour shifts came along!

Late in the fall, Tony and I would leave our cabins in the dark for our night shift. As we walked by the other houses, we could see everybody sitting inside by the fire. We'd climb into an old 1932 Ford truck that didn't even have windows in it and drive eight miles up to the mining site. It was usually snowing and always cold.

Changing shifts at Sixty Mile. The 8R D8 cats
worked 22 hours a day, seven days a week.

When we got off shift in the morning, we'd split lots of wood. The women couldn't split it because it was stunted spruce and just like a corkscrew. One tree we found was three feet high, a foot across at the butt, and twisted up just like an upside down ice-cream cone.

After breakfast one foggy morning I was out on the woodpile when I noticed my dog, Jack, looking across the tundra. I looked. A moose was coming down out of the fog. I grabbed Tony's 30-30 Marlin rifle. I ran up through the yard. The mechanic asked, "What are you after?"

"There's a moose heading across the flat and he'll probably come across the creek above camp," I said.

"Jump on the running board of my pickup," he said. "I'll drive you part way."

I rode a short way and got off. I couldn't see the moose anymore. I walked quietly up the road. Then I saw him about 150 yards away across the creek. I lined up on him, fired, and down he went. Jack tore after him. I jumped off the road and down the bank, but when I crossed the creek I tripped and fell into the mud. I jumped up and ran up the other bank.

The dog had the moose by the head, growling, as the moose tried to get up. I ran over, pumped another shell into the magazine, put the barrel about a foot from the moose's head, and pulled the trigger. God! My ears started ringing so bad. I didn't know what happened. The moose fell back like it was dead. I got my knife out and cut its throat.

Just then the mechanic came up. "You got him, eh?" he asked. "But what the hell did you do to the gun?"

He picked it up. I couldn't believe my eyes. There was no barrel left on it. It had blown right off. There were just two pieces of metal six inches long, one folded to the left and one to the right, at the end of the stock. It's no wonder my ears were ringing so loud. If it had blown up a little farther back it would have killed me. I don't know why the moose died when I pulled the trigger.

The mining season was coming to a close. The days were getting shorter, and it was getting colder. Tony and his wife, Betty, decided to come back to Terrace with Marj and me. I had bought a 1938 one-ton truck from the mechanic to haul the household goods. It was cold and snowing on the day the camp closed down. We were pretty happy to be leaving. Unfortunately, Betty was not well and had to stay in the hospital at Dawson City.

We drove to Boundary, Alaska, which was west on a really rough road. We stayed there that night and in the morning headed out to Tok Junction on the Alaska Highway. We arrived in Whitehorse, and while we waited for Betty to fly down from Dawson, Tony bought a new 1952 Ford Sedan for their trip south.

At night we'd go to the '98 Bar to have a few drinks and talk to the locals. We met a pilot who was flying an old Fairchild. He told us about all the cats collected in areas along the Canol Pipeline.

The Canol ran 600 or 700 miles across country between Norman Wells, N.W.T., and Whitehorse, Yukon. The Americans

*Marj Fosbery in the 1938 one ton-Ford truck,
returning to Terrace in 1952 from Sixty Mile. Steamboat
Mountain on the Alaska Highway is in the background.*

had built it, along with a refinery in Whitehorse so they'd have fuel for their war machinery. Of course the war with the Japanese was long over, and now the cats and trucks along the pipeline were going to be taken back to the States. This fellow said, "There's about 500 cats in one place. In another few weeks, when it freezes up, I could fly out there on skis."

Tony and I were interested in getting into the cat business, so we thought we might go out and pick out a couple of good ones. He said there were also lots of tools, parts, and fuel. We'd have to walk them out over frozen rivers and muskeg for about 300 miles to the Alaska Highway. It would be quite an adventure, but as luck would have it, we didn't have much money or time and we were both married, so we decided against it.

We all headed south, and as we ground our way down the Alaska Highway it got colder and colder. The heater in the old truck didn't work very well.

We stayed over in Dawson Creek, and one evening while we were at a movie, Jack disappeared. We hunted for him for a day and a half. I was almost ready to leave him. Finally we saw him coming out from a farm, looking pretty tired and chewed up. We were sure glad to have him back.

We arrived in Terrace and moved back into our old house. It was the fall of 1952 and the strike was over. I got a job with Postak and MacDonald. They were contracting for Columbia Cellulose, logging big spruce and cottonwooods on the islands of the Skeena between Terrace and Prince Rupert. I was going to be running an old 8R D8.

I drove down to the camp early on Monday morning. There weren't any lights on yet, so I went down into the bush and found the cat. It was sure an old-timer. I checked the oil and the fuel in the starting engine and the main tank. Then I stood on the track and pulled on the crank, which came up through the top of the hood. I wanted to have the cat warmed up by the time the crew came. I cranked and I cranked. It would not start. All I got was a bunch of blisters.

The boss, Neil MacDonald, came along and said, "No. No. You'll never get it going that way. Didn't you notice that the starting motor is all black?"

I had a flashlight and I had seen that it was sooty. He went to his truck and got half a can of gas. He came back, pulled the wires off the sparkplugs to the mags, and threw the gas onto the starting engine. He lit a match and threw it at the engine and "whoof"! Flames shot into the air. Then he put the wires back on, climbed up, gave the crank one pull, and it started. I worked for them all winter.

In June I had an offer to work for Skoglund Logging. Skoglund had bought two International TD18 cats. The boss asked me if I wanted to run one of them with a cable dozer on it. I guess he'd heard that I could operate a blade pretty well. They were into logging and road construction and were building a new railroad grade from Terrace to Kitimat. At that time there was just a trail between the two places that people used to walk in the early days. The only way into Kitimat was by floatplane. Of course, there wasn't anything there until Alcan started to build the aluminum plant.

We sold the old house and moved into one of Bruce Johnson's cabins at Lakelse. I had to leave home at three o'clock in the morning, cross the lake in a boat, and climb 200 feet up the hillside to get on the grade.

There were cats everywhere. Campbell and Bennett had the contract, and they had a lot of old D8s. There were other people working there, too, so whenever I arrived in the dark, it was hard to find where the previous shift had left the cat.

There were some rock bluffs, straight up and down, that the grade had to go through. One day the foreman came along and said, "We're going to move up to those bluffs and we have to get a compressor right up on top."

The top was 300 or 400 feet up from the grade on one side, and the lake was a few hundred feet down on the other side. Jack Foster, a great friend of mine, was running the other TD18. The foreman continued, "You guys take those two cats, get that compressor, and make some sort of tote road. Climb right to the top and park that big blue brute of a compressor up there."

We got it done. He came along again and said, "Now see the grade stakes way down there at the edge of that bluff? We'll ravel out some hoses and get some jackhammers and air down there. We'll do some drilling so we can blast out a little shelf. Tomorrow you'll get one of those cats down there and muck it out. Then we'll have a face to work on, and we'll get an airtrack down there and away we go."

The next day Jack and I looked the situation over. They had blasted the rock, making a small shelf. We couldn't go straight down over the bluff to the shelf because it was just too steep. We decided that Jack would position his cat on top, we'd hook our main lines together, and he'd slowly let me down over the side.

When I got the cat to the loose material, it was a vertical wall, so whenever I made one push out I was hanging on the wall like a spider. We had to have both winches winding to pull me back a few feet so I could get the blade into it again. The cat was hanging straight down. I had to get enough room to turn it crosswise. Of course while he was hanging onto me, I couldn't turn it. I finally got a little hole scratched out, making just enough room for the cat, and eventually I moved enough rock so that I could unhook, turn the cat, and muck out along where the grade would be.

When my shift was over, I left the cat sitting on that little ledge. In the morning, when I shone my flashlight up there, the cat was still in the same place. The whole night shift had gone through and hadn't used it.

I went up to see what I could do. Jack wasn't around, so I couldn't go back up the bluff. I looked over the side. It was about 200 feet down. I didn't think I could make it that way, although there was a lot of material there that they'd blasted. They were ready to blast again. The powderman said, "What are we going to do with this cat? We've got to get it out of here."

At about eight o'clock, along comes the superintendent. He said, "Huh! I thought this cat was out of here last night. It's got to go right now. I'm going to check on the right-of-way up ahead and when I come back I want to see you down on the bottom."

He laughed and walked away. I looked at it and looked at it. I thought I might try to go down backwards. Then I decided to try it frontwards. At least I'd have the blade in front of me if I hit anything. If I could keep the cat going straight down through the rocks and trees and stumps, maybe I'd be okay.

I went over the side. As the cat tipped down, I saw the oil pressure disappear and away we went. It just shot down there. It started to go sideways and then it came back the other way. I continued back and forth until I was halfway down. By then

Tex on a D8 cat, heading for an island on the
Skeena River where they were doing some logging.

there were some rocks and stumps in front of me, so I was able
to creep on down to the bottom. That was sure one of the thrills
of my life!

I worked through that summer of 1953. In September I quit.
I had a brand new Chev pickup. We didn't have the house
anymore, so we decided to go to Vancouver and buy a brand
new sixteen-foot trailer. It seemed like a monstrous thing. We
towed it back to Terrace—a three-day trip over a pretty rough
road. We set our trailer up on the bench, and I went back to
work for Postak and MacDonald driving the old D8.

There were a lot of thrills on that job, too. We were logging
on the islands and had to ford some deep channels. Sometimes
there was only a foot of the cat's hood sticking out of the water.
We always wondered if the old thing would quit out there or get
hung up on a big rock. We didn't have a boat, so the crew would
have had to climb onto the canopy and stay there until I could
get across. I worked there all winter.

7

In Business With Tony
(1954-1955)

In spring 1954 I heard about a cat that was for sale. It was an old 8R D8. The story was that a fellow had taken it from the Alaska Highway project. It was an old army cat that he'd managed to bring down to Terrace. He had apparently traded it in on a new D7 from Finning Tractor. There was no Finning dealer in Terrace at that time. They had a marine outlet in Prince Rupert and tractor shops in Prince George and Vancouver. The price of the cat was $10,000, as is and where is. I went out and had a look at it and fired it up. It was about the same as Neil MacDonald's cat, maybe a little better.

I decided to go to the Bank of Nova Scotia. The new manager was from Nova Scotia and had just opened the branch a few days earlier. I said I'd like to get a loan. Finning's wanted half down on the cat, so I needed $5,000. The bank manager said, "No, if you can come up with 2,500, I'll give you the other 2,500."

I wrote to my dad and asked if he'd loan me the money. I told him that I had a job for it with MacDonald's. They were going logging up on the Portland Canal and said they'd keep the cat busy all summer. The pay was ten dollars an hour; plus they'd supply the fuel and pay my way up there. My dad sent the money. It was March 9, 1954, my first day in business.

We arranged that on Sunday I'd walk the cat down to Shames. There was about a month's work to do there before heading up the Portland Canal. On Saturday I was walking down the street with two friends when I suddenly blacked out and fell to the sidewalk. The next thing I knew I was in the hospital with my friends holding me up. Dr. Mills came up to me and pushed his fingers straight into my solar plexus. I doubled up and went right down on the floor. He said to the boys, "Just leave him here."

I had hepatitis. I was worried because I had payments starting the next day and here I was in hospital. I might be here for a month and then not be able to work for three more months. Things looked pretty bad.

I told Marj to get in touch with Tony. He was working for Finning's in Vancouver. I offered him a 50-50 deal in the business if he'd come up and run the cat. He said he'd do it.

Tony told me later that he arrived at Ford's Cove with the cat in the middle of the night. There was just a wall of timber right down to the beach and mountains straight up all around. They pushed the barge in at high tide and tied it to some trees. When the tide went out, the edge of the barge was fifteen feet above the ground. There was no way to get the cat down.

They decided to turn the cat around, fall some trees, and use the cat's winch to pull enough trees up to the barge to make a ramp. When the ramp was about three feet from the edge, Tony backed the cat over the end. He improved the ramp and they unloaded the trucks and supplies onto the beach. The next day another barge came in with a ramp built right onto it.

When I finally got out of the hospital, I got a job pumping gas for a dollar an hour. One afternoon the fellow in the office came out and said, "Somebody is trying to get hold of you through some sort of radio and telephone connection."

I took the phone and listened. "Need a sprocket." That was all I could get from the message that was coming from somebody on a fishboat up on the Portland Canal.

I hung up, thinking, "Where am I going to get a sprocket? I don't have any money."

Then I remembered an old Caterpillar 75 that I'd seen in the bush down at Shames. It was a forerunner of ours. I got in touch with Finning's in Vancouver and asked if the sprockets would be the same. They said they were, so I went down and looked at it. It was all overgrown with brush. It didn't have any tracks and was sitting down in the silt.

I cleaned the brush away and brought down a big Gilchrist jack. I managed to jack it up and work at it until I got one of the sprockets clear of the swing frame. I needed a puller to get that sprocket off, but I didn't have one. I looked underneath and undid the bolts of the cover on the bottom of the final drive. Then I got the bright idea of sticking some dynamite in there.

I scrounged some dynamite and caps and went back down to the cat. I made a paste out of the dynamite and packed it in way up around the bull gear. Then I put in a cap and a long fuse, packed the rest of the cavity with dirt, and put the cover back.

While I was doing all this, Neil MacDonald's dad came along. He was a rough, tough old Scotsman with a black patch over one eye. He asked what I was doing, and I told him. He said, "Well, you just be careful. My chicken house is not far from here, and I don't want you to scare my chickens and I sure don't want any of them killed!"

I said, "Oh, I'm pretty sure that won't happen. Anyway, I'm ready to light the fuse."

He was kind of skeptical about it, but he went back to his house. I lit the fuse and went behind a big cottonwood tree. I peeked out and pretty soon there was a big boom. The whole thing jumped up in the air along with a cloud of smoke. I couldn't see for all the dust and smoke. When it cleared, I went over and looked. It had blown the whole side off the case. The sprocket was lying on the ground, separate from the hub. All that held it was a bearing on the very end of the hub.

Mr. MacDonald came over and had a look around. Shrapnel had gone every which way through the bushes. He was mighty concerned, and so was I. We went over to look at the chickens. They didn't seem too upset.

I thought, "Holy smoke. I'm pretty good at this. I'll just put a bit of powder under that bearing and blow it off the sprocket instead of beating it off."

I packed the dynamite, wrapped it up with a cap and fuse, lit it, and went behind the tree. Boom! I went over to pick up the sprocket and throw it in the back of my truck. I couldn't believe my eyes. The bearing hadn't moved and the sprocket had blown back up onto the spline. It was off, and now it was back on!

I had to wrestle the hub and sprocket onto the back of my truck. I was still recuperating from my sickness, and it was very heavy. I decided that since I had to take it to Rupert to ship out on a fishboat, I'd stop at the drydock. They had some big presses, so I'd get them to press it off. It took 90 tons to get that sprocket off the spline!

Tony also had problems. He needed pullers to get what was left off the spline because all the spokes were broken, so he skilfully cut it off with a cutting torch and drove the replacement on with a sledgehammer.

One day I got a message that if I was well enough, I should come to Rupert. I could take Postak and MacDonald's D8, which had been in the Finning shop for repairs, onto a barge and up to Ford's Cove. We'd spend the rest of the season working there. Marj was pregnant and wasn't feeling so great, so she decided not to come up to camp with me. Instead, she'd stay in the house we'd rented in Terrace.

I brought the little trailer down from Terrace to Prince Rupert and loaded it on the barge. Then I walked the cat down First Avenue out to Seal Cove. It was blacktop, so I kept one track on the shoulder and had a couple of guys putting planks under the other. It was about a mile and a half, so it took awhile.

We loaded it on the barge, and that night a tug hooked on and towed us out of the harbour. There they unhooked the barge and let us out on a thousand-foot line. It was about an inch and an eighth cable. Then they started towing us up the Portland Canal, about a ten-hour trip to Ford's Cove.

Lou, a faller, was also on the barge with me. We planned to sleep in my trailer that night. It was pitch black. All we could see was the little navigation light on the tug. The only sound was the swish of the water as we were pulled through it. We could feel the vibration of the towline.

When I woke up early in the morning, there was no vibration. I got up and looked out. It was still pitch black, but now I couldn't even see the tug light. And we weren't moving. We were adrift!

I woke Lou and asked him what he thought, but he also had no idea what was going on. We made breakfast. When daylight finally came, we looked out and saw no tug. What the hell could have happened to it? We had no way of finding out or of getting off the barge. And where would we go? We didn't even know where we were. There was no wind, so the barge wasn't moving in any direction.

About ten o'clock we heard an airplane. A floatplane came over the barge, landed about a mile and a half away, and taxied in behind an island.

We wondered what was going on. We waited another hour and saw the plane take off. Pretty soon, out from behind the island came the tug. He came straight over to us. "I guess you were wondering what's been happening," the captain said.

"Yeah, we sure were," I answered.

"We broke down," he said. "We radioed Rupert for an airplane to bring us parts. Now we're underway again."

They picked up the line, put it on the towbit, and away we went. We arrived at Ford's Cove in the afternoon.

The timber sales there belonged to the superintendent and the manager of Nelson Brothers' Fisheries. Postak and MacDonald were the contractors who took the logs out to the booming ground and boomed them.

Logging at Ford's Cove on the Portland Canal, 22 miles south of Stewart, B.C.

We started logging right there on the beach, but it was too soft, so we moved to the creek bottoms. They were full of boulders. The fallers would drop the trees and we'd skid them down the creekbed. You certainly wouldn't do that today.

They finally realized that it was hopeless, so they brought in a high-lead operation from Vancouver Island. They cold-decked the logs and we corduroyed roads across the mud to the cold-deck piles. We skidded them part way on the corduroy, then into the creek bottoms and into the bay at Ford's Cove.

Tony was running our cat, and I was running Postak and MacDonald's. Even though theirs had been overhauled, it still kept breaking down. Ours wasn't very good either. Those boulders were tough on the running gear. We both had big logging arches that we pulled behind the cats.

They had a pile driver come in and build the booming ground. They also drove the piles for the stiff-leg, which is a type of sidewalk, out to the low-tide line. The stiff-leg is made up of a series of boom sticks fastened together "endo" and then secured to the pilings. It was about 300 feet long and provided a place for airplanes and boats to tie up.

Marj was feeling better by now and had flown up to camp on a Queen Charlotte Airlines Fairchild 24 on floats. She was about six months pregnant. Six weeks after she arrived, she became very sick. Her brother Allen was working there as a faller, and

Fosbery Bros.' first cat, a 1938 8R D8, pulling a Carco logging arch down by the log boom at Ford's Cove.

we realized that we had to get her out to the hospital at Stewart. We put Marj on a stretcher and got up on the stiff-leg. There was a hell of a sea running. Even with our caulk-boots we were barely able to keep our footing. We carried her almost to the end, where the fishboat waited. She made that 22-mile trip in very rough seas. Unfortunately she lost the baby after her arrival. Marj returned to Terrace and waited there for the next few months until we finished working at Christmas.

We had a tough time up there. The southwesters would blow in, break up the booming ground, and we'd lose the logs. The rollers on our cat started to go, so I made a trip out to get some replacements. Queen Charlotte Airlines had a Norseman flying up and down the Portland Canal and I got a ride with him.

That's when I first got the idea of flying a floatplane. The pilot dropped me off at Seal Cove and I watched him fly away. I said to myself, "If it's the last thing I do, I'm going to fly a floatplane."

Everyone was pretty downhearted back at the job. The breakdowns were a real problem. One day Neil MacDonald came to us and said, "You know, we're going behind. We can't afford to pay you for your cat. If you want to carry on, maybe someday down the road we'll be able to, but not now. We can't even afford to fix our cat. We can pay your wages if you'll stay and work, but that's all."

Tony and I talked it over. We weren't making much in wages, but it would make the payments. We decided to stay. We couldn't afford to hire a barge to haul us out anyway.

I was glad that Tony was a good mechanic, because I don't think I could have kept that old cat going. He'd been around those old D8s quite a bit. Many nights we were out all night patching and welding so we could work the next day.

It was late in the fall, all the equipment was parked, and the high-lead fellows had gone. There was just the two of us left. No barge ever came. The snow kept falling. We were still skidding out of the cold-deck piles. It looked awfully hopeless. We didn't know what we should be doing.

Finally we got word that a barge was coming just before Christmas so that we could load up their equipment and our cat and trailers. The barge came in during a blinding snowstorm. There was already six feet of snow on the ground. We worked all night at low tide, loading the barge so we could go out on high tide the next day.

That old D8 of ours was the only thing still running. We had to push or pull all the other equipment onto the barge. We were sure glad to get back down to Rupert. We unloaded everything onto the dock, took our trailers, and went home to Terrace.

After Christmas, Neil came to see us. He'd managed to find some money and paid us a fair bit of change. We had the cat hauled by train to Terrace and got ready to overhaul it. We rented an old army shop behind the Legion, moved our welder into it, and bought some welding rod.

I had worked on the railroad grade the year before, and I knew that there were places where Campbell and Bennett had overhauled their old 8Rs, leaving lots of parts—better than ours—in dumps alongside the railroad.

We put the cat in the shop, pulled the swing frames off, turned them upside down, and pulled all the rollers off. They were three-piece rollers and they were all just hanging there like cow bells.

We had to throw them away. They had made a single shell roller too, and I knew that there were some of those out at the dumps.

The railroad was running only a way-freight through to Kitimat at that time. We arranged, for a bottle of whiskey, to ride out on the caboose every so often. They'd stop at the dumps, and we'd get off with our snow shovels, sleigh, and lunches.

There was about six feet of snow, so we'd dig and dig until we hit some iron. Then we'd scratch around and find rollers, sprockets, and idlers. They were worn, but we could still use them. We'd load them on the sleigh, dig a trail up the bank, and pull them up to the tracks.

The train came back around midnight. We'd have a big fire going, and they'd stop while we loaded our stuff onto the flatcar. Then we'd climb into the caboose and ride to Terrace, load our stuff onto our truck, and go home to bed.

The next day we'd unload and sort our wares. We took the rollers apart and rebuilt them and did the same with the idlers and sprockets. We did lots of welding. We used almost 900 pounds of welding rod on that old girl. We didn't have money to buy parts for the rest of it. It needed new steering clutches, and although the engine ran all right, it didn't have much power.

About five o'clock one night in March 1955, the shop door opened and in stepped the superintendent of Columbia Cellulose. He said, "I'm looking for a cat for tomorrow. We've got to do some snowploughing down at Remo and Shames, but I see this one's not ready to go." Both swing frames were still upside down on each side of it. He said, "I'll have to go look for another one."

I said, "We'd sure like that job."

"Yeah, but you're not ready to go," he said.

"What time tomorrow?" I asked.

"Eight o'clock in the morning."

"We'll be ready," I said.

He went out the door shaking his head. We went down to the beer parlour at the Terrace Hotel. We knew lots of guys who hung around there hadn't worked for a long time. "We'll supply the beer if you come and help us tonight," I said.

We worked all night. At eight o'clock she was sitting outside, puffing away. The lowbed pulled up and away we went to work for Columbia Cellulose. We were happy to be working, especially at ten dollars an hour.

We knew the old cat's days were numbered. One day I told Lloyd Evans, the woods supervisor, that we'd ordered a new D8, but we wouldn't get it for a while yet.

In the spring we went up on the Kalum River. They wanted to dredge it so they could drive logs down it again. The water was right up to the deck all the time, so we were working underwater. When I went over the bank, I didn't see the blade again until I came out the other side. It was a cable blade and I had no control over it. It just bounced along over the rocks and it might come out with a rock in front of it or not. If I did catch some material, the current would usually wash it away. I wasn't accomplishing much, and the blade was taking a hell of a beating.

One day I saw oil flowing around me. I backed out onto the shore and saw it running out of the final drive. It was nearly Easter, so we'd have a long weekend to fix it. Tony ordered a bellow seal and we got some pullers out of Prince George. By the end of the weekend she was ready to go again.

Lloyd watched me one day while I pushed out a stump. "That's pretty sick," he said. I thought he was going to fire me. "When's that new one coming?" he asked.

"Soon I hope," I answered.

He said, "I hope so, too."

Before we'd ordered the D8, we knew that the TD24s would be available anytime. We decided to talk to the B.C. Equipment salesman in Terrace about trading the old 8R on a new TD24. He came out and looked at her and got in touch with his boss in Prince George. The next week he came out to the job and said, "They tell me that we can't deal with you."

"Why's that?" I asked.

"They thought you were a poor risk, with this old cat and just getting started," he said.

We were pretty upset with Finning's, but we went back to them anyway, to try to make a deal. They said they'd get us a 14A D8, but it might take awhile. I limped along all summer with that old girl. Tony and Betty had gone back to the Yukon to work for Harold Schmidt at Ballarat Creek, so I didn't have him to help me with repairs. Somehow I managed to keep her going. One steering clutch was slipping so bad that I had to turn it around with one track. I'd go ahead and back up and go ahead. As long as it was pushing straight ahead and I didn't touch the steering clutch, it was okay, but if I'd hit the clutch it would have slipped and never held again.

One day I was walking it to another site where I was building landings on the mountainside for some high-lead loggers. I went over a rock and "bang!"—the whole engine fell onto the ground right between the tracks. The main spring had broken in half.

I remembered that there was a spring in the old 75 at Shames, so I went down and jacked it up once more. I brought its spring up to my cat, and there on the side of the road I jacked up the front, pulled out the broken one, and put in the other. It weighed about 500 pounds, and even though I had a fellow helping me, it was a tough job.

8

Opening Up Northwestern B.C.
(1955-1958)

In September, Finning Tractor let me know that they had our brand new super 14A D8 cat in Kitimat. It had come from Peoria, Illinois, to Vancouver by train and then up the coast on a barge. On Sunday we drove down to look at it. It was absolutely beautiful.

They gave us $5,600 for the old one, and the new one cost $41,000. It was a whole bunch of money, but I had a pretty steady job at sixteen dollars an hour.

That was the beginning. Along with a few other contractors, I spent the winter building the main road from Terrace up to the Nass River. In the spring, along comes a fellow I'd never seen before. He said he was the new company manager and he was shutting this job down. So there I was, out of a job.

That was 1956. Tony was back again, so we went over to Kitimat. Construction had started there in 1950, and it was still going strong. We were hired by Lakelse Construction, one of Ray Skoglund's companies. Tony and I were double-shifting, and a few weeks later Ray said that if we had another cat, he'd hire it, too.

Finning's said they had a good used 13A, so we bought it. We double-shifted both cats and by fall we were in pretty good shape. The company gave us a contract to do the section of right-of-way between Humphrey Creek and the Kitimat River. They built us some bunkhouses on sleighs. Tony and I moved the camp about fifteen miles up on the existing right-of-way and made a campsite beside a creek. It was near Christmas by then. We left an oil stove going in one of our trailers because we planned to come out between Christmas and New Year's Day. We were going to make a cat road of about twelve miles, connecting our side with the Lakelse side.

We caught the train from Kitimat to Terrace and spent Christmas with our families. My dad and his wife Helen had come up from Lumby, and they said they'd like to come with us when we went back to camp. We said it would be rough riding on those cats, but they really wanted to come and we were glad to have them.

On December 27 we caught the train to Kitimat, fired up the cats, loaded up Dad, Helen, their dog, and one suitcase, and rattled our way to camp. We arrived at about one o'clock in the morning. It had snowed steadily since we left, so there was about three feet on the ground.

I took the flashlight and opened the door to the trailer where we'd left the oil stove going. I shone the light inside. It was like looking into a black tunnel. The whole place was covered in about four inches of oily soot! It was hanging from the ceiling like big black icicles. The stove was still going. We never did figure out just what had happened.

We were cold and wet, so we opened up one of the bunkhouses and went to bed. Early the next morning we fuelled up, put Helen and the dog and suitcase on with Tony, and Dad with me, and headed out. We figured we could punch that twelve-mile tote road through okay.

The snow and monstrous windfalls and heavy second-growth didn't let us make very good time. We managed to cross the Kitimat River in the daylight, but the bank was so steep on the other side that we couldn't climb out. Tony had to push me up and then I winched him up.

It was nearly dark and we still had five miles of heavy bush and a mountainside ahead of us. We didn't have the time to go back to camp and try again the next day. We decided to leave the cats and walk on the original Indian trail to Lakelse Lake. When we started out we could see the blazes on the trees. When it got dark we used our flashlights. Soon our batteries were dead and we had to try to feel for the marks on the trees.

It continued to snow. Tony and I took turns carrying the German Shepherd pup and the suitcase and breaking trail. By that time we had nothing left to eat, so we were pretty hungry. At about three o'clock in the morning we saw some light through the trees. It was the end of the right-of-way coming from the north that we'd been looking for.

For the next four miles we walked on the tote road, which was much easier. We came to the hot springs area where the warm temperature had melted the snow away. We threw ourselves down onto the bare ground, just about finished. There was an old crank-style telephone hanging in a tree at the end of the Lakelse telephone line about a mile away, so Tony went to call Betty, in Terrace, to come and get us. The phone was dead!

We had to walk another mile to Bruce Johnson's place on the lake. It was coming daylight when we got there. There were cars coming out of his yard after the holiday celebrations. The people were sure surprised to see us. They gave us a ride sixteen miles back to Terrace. We got to my place at nine in the morning. All of us were dead tired, including the pup. There was a bottle of rum on the counter. Tony and I drank the whole thing and passed out.

A few days later we hired one of Columbia Construction's cats to push a road to our cats. We brought them up to where there was truck access. A couple of days after that, with two fallers and two chokermen, we headed to our camp. As Tony was crossing the Kitimat River, his cat slid into a big hole. The water was right up over the fan. The men, bedrolls, and grub, all of which were riding on the cat, slipped into the icy water.

The women and kids came on the train to Kitimat a few days later, and we brought them up to the camp on the cat. Our daughter Jan was a baby at that time. Marj did the cooking and Betty helped her. They didn't have the modern facilities that they had in Terrace, but they enjoyed camp life.

We had a few problems through that winter. One day we blew an "O" ring on the 14A's hydraulic system. I noticed that one of the men had a worn spot in his watch pocket that could have been made from a contraceptive device. I said, "Pop it out and we'll see if it will work as an 'O' ring." We cut the end out of it. It fit perfectly and lasted all winter. In the spring I told Finning's that the only way we could keep their equipment running was with French safes and haywire.

We finished that job, loaded everybody and all our gear onto the cats, and went through the bush to meet up with Columbia Construction's cats coming from the Terrace side. Ours were the first machines that ever went between Kitimat and Terrace.

The next summer we went to the Queen Charlotte Islands to build a road between Port Clements and Masset. The cats and pickups were taken by barge, and Tony and I flew over with our families on Queen Charlotte Airlines. We flew from the harbour at Rupert in a PBY and landed at the airport at Sandspit.

We were there until fall, pushing mud around. It was another kind of world. A lot of the people didn't do much. We called it the land of no hurry and no worry.

One day in the fall we were servicing our cats at the end of the shift when we thought we heard some kind of engine. There were no fallers around because the timber was so small that we'd just smash it down and push it aside. In a few minutes a TD24 came out of the brush and up onto our grade. There were men hanging all over it. The operator spun her around and shut her down.

One of them said, "We're glad we caught you. We're working from the Masset end and we want to spend the long weekend in Port Clements."

We took them down with us, and on Monday we came back up to get ready for work the next day. Pretty soon they came along in the back of a government dump truck, jumped off, and started up the TD24. I was working on my cat about 50 feet away. When the dump truck turned around to go back to Port Clements, I saw that it didn't have a tailgate. I also noticed that there was a guy lying crosswise in the back. When the truck shot ahead, the guy rolled to the back, and when it backed up, he rolled to the front.

The driver was having a hard time turning around in the mud. He went back and forth a few more times, and the guy rolled right out onto the ground. I jumped up to run over because I could see what was going to happen. I ran toward him, yelling for the driver to stop, but I was too late. He backed up and stopped. The guy's head was in the mud with the dual tires on top of it.

When the driver heard what had happened, he just about had a fit. He got the truck moved ahead and we pulled the guy out. He was a big Cree Indian fellow, passed out. One of the boys said, "Oh, we forgot about him."

They brought the cat over and put him up over the hood, between the exhaust pipes. Away they all went, hanging onto the cat, drinking beer, and singing.

The next afternoon I was working when I saw this same great big guy walking out of the bush. I couldn't believe my eyes. His shirt was ripped off, he had blood and burn marks all over him, and the imprint of the tire was still on his face. He said, "I was on the cat and I guess I fell off."

Everybody was so drunk they didn't even know he was gone. I said, "If you can handle it till quitting time, we'll take you to the outpost hospital at Port Clements."

The nurse patched him up, and the next day he caught a fishboat and went around Rose Spit to Masset and finally got back on the job.

We enjoyed being on the Queen Charlottes. We used to say that when the tide was out, the table was set. There were all kinds of things to eat on the beaches and in the sea. There were also thousands of small deer. Every Monday night on the way home from work we'd shoot one and share it.

Later on, to make it more interesting, we started going out after dark to get one. There were so many eyes shining around those meadows. Some were deer and some were raccoons. One night we had a buck lined up to shoot. Tony said, "Turn the lights off. I'm going to see if I can sneak up and catch him."

He did get hold of him, but that deer was too tough for Tony. He flipped him off and was gone.

Another night we had shot our deer and were driving home through the meadows and grassy hills. We could drive anywhere around there close to the ocean. We saw eyes shining from up in a tree. We stopped. My old dog, Jack, loved hunting. I climbed up the tree and chased a raccoon down. Jack grabbed him as he hit the ground. That didn't last long. The coon had Jack by the lip and he wasn't letting go. Jack couldn't fight back. He just lay there and howled. We couldn't hit the coon with a club because we might hit the dog. Finally we shot him in the head right beside my dog's head. Old Jack wasn't so interested in hunting coons after that.

One day I was driving down to Queen Charlotte City for some parts. There was a big storm blowing. It was just like a snowstorm, with the foam flying off the waves, across the road, and into the timber. I stopped at the edge of some high bluffs to eat my lunch. I never saw such a sight. Fifty-foot waves were crashing onto the beach below. The pickup was rocking so bad I could hear the front springs squeaking. I heard later that at Sandspit the wind was blowing at 90 miles per hour.

In the fall we went back to the mainland. We sent our cats, shovel, and pickups on a little barge and we went on the *Camosun*, a 10,000-ton CPR steamship. We weren't out an hour before the waves were washing over the lower deck. Twenty minutes later they were over the second deck. We were up in the observation room and all we could see was green water. The ship was going straight down and then straight up. The piano in the lounge was crashing into the walls, and the ship sounded like it was coming apart.

Soon there wasn't a soul in sight. I was the only one of our group who wasn't sick. I was down in our cabin and I thought about our poor dogs in the rope locker on the main deck. I asked one of the crew how I could get up there. He said there was a tube with a ladder up through the three levels. As I climbed, the wind became louder, and by the time I reached the main deck it was a roar.

Those dogs were so sick. The green slime was running out of them and water was coming in on them through the cracks. There was nothing I could do, so I just talked to them awhile before I had to leave. It was sure a wild night in Hecate Strait.

When we woke up in the morning, we were tied up in the harbour at Prince Rupert. I noticed that the ship was listing pretty badly to port. The cargo had all shifted in the storm.

It was December 1957 when we got back to Terrace. I had bought a lot on Olson Road the year before and had made arrangements with a fellow to build a house while we were in the Charlottes. It wasn't finished, but he promised that it would be by Christmas.

We were quite excited to be moving into a brand new house. On Christmas Eve we had some people over for a few drinks. I hung Jan's sock over the fireplace, and the fire was burning merrily away when suddenly we heard a "whoof" and the fire disappeared! There was a cloud of smoke and steam, but no more flames or wood.

I went over and looked and there was just a big hole and some embers down on the ground. The bottom had fallen right out of the fireplace.

The ground was muddy, so the fire went out quickly. We patched up the hole to keep the wind from blowing through the house. We could laugh about it later, but not that night.

In the spring, the roof developed a bad leak. I went up and shovelled the snow and swept the water off. I couldn't find the leak, so I decided to drill a hole in the floor and put a piece of garden hose in it. Then I got a bucket and my 30-06. I shot a hole in the ceiling to line up with the one in the floor. Of course the water came pouring through into the bucket. When it quit, I went up on the roof and drilled the hole to fit the hose. I pushed the hose up through the hole and sealed around it with tar. The water ran right through onto the ground after that.

Once we got the fireplace fixed and a new aluminum roof on the house, we lived there quite comfortably for many years.

That winter we logged cottonwoods and spruce on the bars along the Skeena River for Western Plywood. Tony ran the cat and I set chokers. We had a faller and a fellow on the boom. We made our booms up on the bars instead of in the water. Dry-booms were made in the same way as wet-booms. When they were finished, we hooked a one-and-an-eighth-inch cable onto the corner of the boom and tied it to a tree. When high water came, the boom would float. The tugs came from Rupert, pushed the booms up to get some slack, undid the hook, and towed the booms away.

When there was enough water in the spring we'd wet-boom, stowing the logs in the booms with boats. A fellow upriver had borrowed one of our boats with an eighteen-horsepower motor on it. When he was done with it, I decided to run the boat downriver to our operation.

It was cold, so I put on my coat, mitts, cap, and coveralls. Then I decided to put on my life-jacket for the warmth. We always carried them, but we never wore them.

I got into the boat and opened the throttle. The boat started to porpoise, which meant there was too much weight at the back

The Fosberys: Tex, Bob, Jan, Marj, and Eve at Terrace in 1958.

for the amount of power. We had a dynamite box for a seat, so I pushed it up toward the middle and moved forward. As I did, the boat levelled off, the motor kicked around to the right, and I shot over the side! The throttle was wide open and that boat went crazy. It raced right over top of me. When I came up, it was going in circles down the river.

Ice that had been pushed up by the tide was flowing along beside me. The river was 150 feet wide and I was in the middle. There was a logjam half a mile downstream, and I knew if I got sucked into that it would be the end of me. "Don't panic," I told myself.

I swam as fast as I could without tiring myself out. My clothes were so heavy. Finally I got to the rocks, but I couldn't drag myself out of the river. That was it. I had no more strength, and I was really starting to shake.

Then I heard a train coming. I raised my head. Someone had seen the boat downstream, so it was coming along slowly.

The track was about 60 feet above me. I waited until it got closer, then lifted my arm and waved weakly.

They saw me, stopped the train, and carried me up the bank and into the engine. I asked them to take me to Riv-Tow Tug and Barge at Salvas. I thought I'd catch a ride downriver and pick up my boat. As it happened, I stayed at their base and Tony picked me up that night. I was still shaking from hypothermia.

When we were done on the bars, we went home and overhauled the cats. That was 1958. The IWA was on strike and the forest fire season came along, so there wasn't much work in the bush. We were running cats for Skoglund Logging for awhile, and then the summer grew very hot and dry. Forest fires began springing up everywhere. Suddenly there was lots of work for our cats, building firebreaks up in the Copper River area and the Nass River.

9

Learning to Fly
(1958-1966)

That same summer of 1958 the Vancouver Aero Club brought up two Cessna 140s and ran a satellite flight training school in Terrace. It was my chance to learn to fly.

I took in the ground school and dual flight whenever I wasn't away on fires. One time I was gone for over two weeks, and when I got back they were just about done. I hadn't finished my ground school or done my solo. The instructor said, "We'll work hard and get you through." We went up for a few days doing circuits and stalls, and the second day he said, "Okay, you make a circuit."

As I was rolling down the runway I remember thinking, "What am I doing sitting in this thing all by myself? I don't think I'm ready for this."

I went around, came in, and it was beautiful. The instructor ran over, shook my hand, and congratulated me. He said, "Come over to the terminal and I'll buy you a cup of coffee. Then you can spend the afternoon doing circuits by yourself."

I was feeling pretty good about my flying ability. We had coffee, and I went up again. When I came back I noticed that the windsock was blowing crosswise to the runway. I thought, "Holy lightning! Now what?"

As I got closer to the ground, I could see that I was drifting. I knew I wasn't controlling it properly, but I figured I'd better get the bloody thing down onto the ground. That was my big mistake.

I landed, skipping from one tire to the other, and eventually went right off the runway into the brush and rocks. The plane went into a ground loop. The wing hit the ground and ripped a big hole in it, and the tail wheel got ripped off.

The instructor ran over. He sure wasn't as happy a man as he was the last time he ran over to me. He gave me hell. It was a major thing to fix an airplane this far away from Vancouver.

I had to go to work again for awhile. I did a few more circuits with him later on, but it was never the same. As soon as I got close to the ground I'd be really nervous and just couldn't get onto landing it right. Fall came, and most of the students got their licences, but I didn't get mine. I was determined though, and that winter I hired an instructor who tutored me in ground school.

In April I phoned the Vancouver Aero Club and said I was coming down to buy a floatplane and fly it back. When I got to Vancouver I told them that I wanted to finish my training on a floatplane. The fellow said, "Well, we have an Aeronca Sedan here that we'll sell for $7,000."

I phoned my banker in Terrace and told him what I wanted to do. He said, "I don't think that's such a good plan." He did loan me the money though, and I bought the plane without even having a licence. The fellow said, "We've got a good instructor here. Her name is Helen Harrison."

She was a famous woman pilot. She'd ferried bombers from Labrador to England during the war. She had thousands of hours and lots of time on floats. I learned more from her in two hours than I had from the other instructors in days. After two hours I went solo, and I never looked back. I got my licence on my birthday, April 27, 1959.

I flew back to Terrace, stopping once for fuel at Sullivan Bay. I landed on the Skeena River by the old bridge. I was pretty proud of myself. I remembered Helen saying as I left, "I just hate to think of the places you'll fly in your life from now on."

Now we needed a hangar for our airplane. Dud Little, the mayor of Terrace at the time, had property along the Skeena, so we made arrangements to build one there. It was quite a ways down to the river at low water, so we put in a track. Then we got some four by fours and some old wheels and made a carriage. We hung a block in the centre of the hangar. We'd put the floats onto the carriage, back the pickup along the road, which

Tex and a bear cub he found near Hell's Gate Slough on the Skeena River in 1959.

pulled the cable through the block and the airplane into the hangar. It worked very well.

I flew the airplane to our job sites on the Skeena and the Nass that summer, servicing cats and getting parts. We were the first contractors in the area to have our own aircraft.

During the winter of 1959 we were working across the Skeena from Terrace. We had a 14A D8 skidding logs for Skoglund Logging. We'd skid them down to the riverbank, unhook the chokers from the turn of logs, hook up another set of chokers, and go back to the bush for another turn of logs. The logs on the riverbank were hooked up to a carriage that was connected by a skyline between two spar trees, one on each side of the river. The carriage swung the logs across the river. The home tree on the Terrace side was rigged with a heel-boom, and it loaded the logs onto a truck as they came across.

When the job was finished, I wanted to take the cat back to Terrace to do some work on it. We could take it back the way we'd brought it over, which meant we'd have to walk it through the bush to a CNR siding. Then we'd have to load and block it and tie it down for the five-mile trip to Terrace, unload, and walk it two miles to the shop. The railway wanted $150 for this trip.

I figured we were only about a mile from the shop as the crow flies, and the water was low and clear. I flew over the river to check it out. I decided that I could walk the cat across the river to the Terrace side.

Since the cat was going to be completely submerged, I put an extension on the air cleaner, slacked off the fan belts, plugged the vents on the clutch and transmission, and sealed up the starting motor. I hooked a 200-foot guy line onto my bullhook, so if worse came to worst we could get the cat pulled back to dry land.

I tied a boat onto the canopy and started across the river. By the time I got to the middle, the water was a foot over the cat and only my head and shoulders were sticking out. I started to feel a bit dizzy and couldn't tell if I was still moving. I thought I might be hung up on a big rock. I could feel movement through the seat, and the engine was still running, but I didn't seem to be moving ahead.

Eventually the water level on the canopy began to drop and I felt some relief, figuring that now I'd make it to shore. It was probably a crazy idea but it worked. As far as I know, I was the only person to make that trip across the Skeena River by cat.

In 1960, when Jan was five years old, our daughter Joy came into our lives. I came home from work one weekend, and Marj was looking after a little Indian baby until she could be placed in a permanent home. The following two weekends, when I got home I found the baby still there. I thought she was pretty neat, and although I really wanted a boy, we decided to adopt this little girl. We called her Joy because she was such a happy little thing.

Bob Fosbery with the Aeronca Sedan, the first airplane
owned by Fosbery Bros. It's tied up on the Skeena River in 1960.

In March 1960 my brother-in-law Allen Kennedy and I flew 50 miles down the Skeena River to look at a timber sale at Alder Creek. We circled around and saw where the mouth of the creek ran into a big slough that was part of the river system. The slough pinched out at the mouth of the creek except for a small trickle of water separating a mud flat from the mainland. We landed in the slough and taxied up, hoping to get to the mouth of the creek, but there wasn't enough water. We were about three-quarters of a mile away. There was a stump on the mud flat, about seven feet in diameter and sixteen feet high with a huge mass of roots. We taxied up the channel to it and stopped. I tied a rope onto one side of the airplane, walked around the stump, and tied the end to the other side.

We decided to walk up the island instead of on the mainland, which had a lot of snow and windfalls. The island had been washed pretty clean over the years. There were just a few big spruce and some alders on it.

We took our lunches and the rubber boat to cross the small channels. It got quite warm, so we left our coats with the boat, figuring we'd wade the rest of the channels. We got to the creek mouth, hiked up the mountain for a couple of hours, and then headed back. When we reached the creek mouth, we saw, to our dismay, that everything, including the island, was underwater. I hadn't thought about why there was snow on the mainland and none on the island. Now I realized that we'd landed where the high tide would back up into the river. I learned a good lesson that day.

But there we were, with three-quarters of a mile between us and the airplane—if it was even still there. That stump might have floated away or the rope might have floated to the top and come right off it. Either way, the airplane would be gone. It was almost dark, and there was no way to contact anyone.

I saw a big sweeper about a hundred yards away and said to Allen, "I'm going to walk out on that tree and see how deep the water is."

I made my way through the limbs to the end. I looked down twenty feet into what seemed like about five feet of water. I decided that even if I jumped off and made it to the island, there was still a foot of water over there. We'd be even more wet and miserable. We'd just have to wait and follow the tide as it went out.

We stood under some big spruce trees. I looked down and saw the remains of an old camp fire. There were some matches lying in the ice. I dug them out. I had heard that rubbing them in your hair would eventually dry them out enough to light. We just about wore holes in our heads, but it didn't work.

It got dark and a cold wind began to blow. It was a clear night, so I could see that the tide had finally backed off. We went out on that long spruce, jumped off the end, and landed on bare ground. We started running down the island. When the tide starts to move, it does so quickly. We got to where we'd left the boat. Of course it was gone, along with our coats.

We waded into the water. Immediately, it was up over our belts. We hadn't paid much attention to the depth when we came across that channel with the boat. We went back into the bush and stood behind a spruce, out of the wind. After awhile we got a six-foot-long stick and went down to the water again. I was taller than Allen so I said, "I'll go ahead. If I fall down, just hang onto the stick and I'll pull myself back up." We tried it three times. We couldn't make it. The water was too deep and, my God, it was cold.

Finally, as the tide receded, we made it across and ran down the island toward where we'd left the airplane. As we came out of the buck brush and onto the mud flat, I could see the stump, but no airplane. My heart sank. I looked again, but I couldn't see any airplane.

When we were twenty feet from the stump we spotted it. The fuselage had been lined up behind the stump, but now we could see the wing tips on either side of it.

We ran to the airplane, thinking that it might be full of water, but it was bone-dry inside. We climbed in, lit a candle, and dug into the hardtack. It was one o'clock in the morning. We were so happy to be in the dry cockpit and out of the wind.

Soon we heard the lapping of water against the floats. The tide was coming in again. We could feel the airplane lifting up and floating. We could hear the ice banging against the floats. The tide was pushing it up from the mouth of the Skeena.

After awhile I looked at the luminous dial of the turn-and-bank indicator. I noticed that we were tipping, so I turned on the landing light. The left float was underwater. The rope had hooked onto the bottom of the stump, and the airplane was going up but the rope wasn't. It was tipping us into the stump. I took another piece of rope, choked it around the stump, and tied it onto the dry side. I gave Allen a hunting knife, and while I hung onto his belt and the strut, he reached down into that ice-cold water and cut the other rope.

Now there was 60 feet of rope between the stump and the airplane. We could hear the ice banging into the floats, but we weren't too concerned. We turned the landing light on every once in awhile. Soon it was quiet again, slack tide. There was only a foot of the stump sticking out, so we were in fifteen feet of water. I said, "I hope that stump doesn't shift when the tide goes out."

It was four o'clock in the morning. The airplane started to swing around the stump as the tide receded. We were hanging downstream. The current got faster and the ice was really banging the floats. We wiped the steam off the window and looked out. I saw a big black shape. "What the hell is that?" I asked.

I turned the light on and saw a huge tree coming right at us! Its roots were twice as high as the airplane. "Allen, I've got to make a move," I said, as I jumped out and grabbed the paddle. I paddled as hard as I could until I had the airplane at the very end of the rope. The roots just skimmed by the wingtip. The tree was 150 feet long. I continued to paddle hard to keep away from the limbs. Some of them went under the wing and ripped off the antenna.

Finally it started to come daylight. The tide kept going out. I crawled out to look things over and pumped the water out of the left float. Then I cut the rope tying us to the stump, fired up the engine, taxied out into the main river, and took off.

We landed in Terrace amid lots of activity. There were two airplanes warming up at the airport, ready to start searching for us. A DC3 and another aircraft were about to leave Vancouver to join them. Everybody was glad to see us, and we were certainly happy to be back. It sure taught us that we'd better have a tide book with us when we travelled around the saltchuck.

In 1960 we were working up in the Nass country. We had a brand new 36A D8 and a 14A D8. We ran the machines ourselves. That summer we got rid of the 14A D8, bought another 36A D8, and hired an operator. I would take two weeks off to do business and look for more work. Then I'd go back on the cat and Tony would take time off. In the spring he went down to Cassidy on

Tex with one of the first rippers in that country. The company bought it in the early 1960s from the Diamond Match Co. of Cour d'Alene, Idaho.

Vancouver Island to get his pilot's licence. He trained on a Fleet Canuck.

We decided that we needed a better performing airplane. We sold the Aeronca Sedan on wheels to Bill Sargent, who owned the Inlander Hotel at Old Hazelton. I got the same price as I'd paid for it. The registration was CF-GCO. It crashed later on at Germansen Landing, killing a man and his wife.

We bought a Super Cub, CF-MDY, from Calgary. It had a total time of 150 hours and cost $12,000. We used tundra tires with only four pounds of pressure so we could land on river bars and other rough places.

In March 1964 we had the airplane on wheels. One Sunday I decided to go flying. I flew out around Lakelse Lake and saw that the lake was still frozen and there was a truck driving across it.

After lunch I picked up my friend Peter Dychikowski at the airport. He was the engineer for Transprovincial Air Carriers and one of the best that I ever met. I said, "Let's go out for a fly

and we'll have a cup of coffee at the restaurant at Lakelse Lake."
We flew around the mountains awhile and headed back. "Is that
ice okay?" he asked.

"Oh yeah," I replied. "See that road over there? There was a
truck driving on it this morning."

We landed on the south end and started taxiing along the
shore toward the restaurant. Transprovincial Air had a seaplane
base there, which they used in the summer. We were going along
when all of a sudden we went right through the ice! Green water
and ice was all we saw through the windshield. The airplane was
being held up by the wings on the ice, but the whole front end
was in the water.

There's only one door in a Super Cub, and Peter and I never
did decide who was the first one out. He said it must have been
me because his head was wet and mine wasn't. He figured that I
stepped on his head as I got out!

We walked the hundred yards to shore. Lloyd Johnson, the
owner of Transprovincial Air, came running to meet us. "I
watched you coming in and I knew what was going to happen,"
he said. "That ice was water only a few days ago. It just froze up
and got a little snow on it. The part where the truck had driven
has been frozen since the fall."

I phoned a friend who had a Hiller helicopter, and he flew
over to the lake. I took a rope out to the airplane and tied it
around the propellor. It was bent like the horns of a longhorn
steer. He hovered over me and I hooked the hook into his and
got out of the way.

I'd told him to lift it very slowly so the water could run out. It
was a fabric-covered airplane and the weight would break the
belly open. He lifted it gently, and the water poured out. He swung
it over to solid ice and was just about to let it down when the rope
broke. It went through the ice and broke the belly wide open.

By then Tony had arrived. I grabbed a choker out of the
back of his pickup, went out to the plane, and put a hitch on the

*Fosbery Bros.' Super Cub in the foreground on Lakelse
Lake in 1964. They bought it in Calgary for $12,000.*

prop and around the hub. The helicopter jerked it out of the water and scooted it to shore.

Peter had gone into their shop and brought out a Herman Nelson, which is a big aircraft heater. He had it running on the shore. He stuffed one pipe into the cabin and one into the cowling. He took the mags off and dried them. We used masking tape to bandage up the fuselage, drained the water out of the oil, and put the mags back on. He said, "We'll have this home before dark."

"Peter," I said. "I don't like the looks of that propellor. It's all twisted up."

"Don't worry about it," he said. "If it had a piece missing I'd say no, but it's still in balance. One side is as heavy as the other. It'll get you there."

We fired the plane up and it ran like a top. Just before dark I snuck it along the shore, took off, and climbed up to 4,000 feet. If it quit I'd have enough altitude to go back or to go on to the airport. It flew faster than ever with that bent-up propellor. I came down in a big cloud of sparks. I had no tail-wheel, so I skidded along on the broken springs and arrived at Peter's hangar just at dark.

Tex did lots of flying in the mountains on the north coast of B.C. and had some pretty exciting trips.

Two weeks later, one of Transprovincial Air's Beavers had a similar experience. The pilot, Cedric Mah, was taking some freight to a surveyor's camp on the lake at Meziadin. He was taxiing along about 150 feet from shore when he broke through. There was a creek mouth nearby, and it kept the ice pretty thin.

Tony volunteered to fly up with Peter Dychikowski. They planned to make a tripod and lift the plane up, but the weather was warm and the ice was too thin. They called a company in Winnipeg to fly out some low-profile airjacks, which they put under the wings. They were supported by poles laid on the ice. It took two weeks to finally get that Beaver onto safe ice and running again.

We were closely associated with Transprovincial Air Carriers, which was based at Lakelse Lake. It was a good company with good pilots, but it was tough country, with tough weather for flying. Lloyd Johnson was the key man to the operation. He took in Doug Chappell as the chief pilot, with shares in the company. Their first airplane was a Beaver, registered CF-TPA, which Doug flew back from the factory. I watched him land that spanking new airplane on Lakelse Lake. Then they got a Cessna 180 and two second-hand Beavers from the Ontario Forest Service for

Peter Dychikowski,(top left) engineer for Transprovincial Air Carriers, at Meziadin Lake in 1964. He and a helper are digging out the Beaver after pilot Cedric Mah broke through the thin lice. Air jacks (inflatable bags) were required to help lift the airplane out of the lake and the snow was packed down with snowshoes to make a strip for take-off. It took two weeks to get the Beaver up and running.

$45,000 apiece. There was lots of work, with mining exploration, timber cruising, and the construction of the Stewart-Cassiar Highway. They bought two Otters and leased a Norseman. There were 22 float planes on Lakelse Lake, counting theirs and others. It was an exciting time.

Peter's brother Bill, an experienced pilot, started to fly for them in the summer of 1964. One day he flew out to Trapper Lake to pick up four men and a diamond drill. There are lots of downdrafts in that area, and it was quite windy. He took off, circling the lake to gain altitude because of his heavy load. An Indian fellow watched from the lakeshore. The airplane climbed up, rolled over, and spiralled down into the lake.

Members of Search and Rescue, people from the Ministry of Transport, and the insurance adjustor came from Whitehorse to retrieve the wreckage and the bodies. They made camp, and as they were towing in the wreckage with their boat, they heard gunfire. The camp was in flames and their ammunition was exploding! They released the airplane and raced for shore, but they couldn't salvage much. They spent two days in the body bags, trying to keep warm and waiting for an airplane to return for them. It started to freeze up, so they left the wreckage until the following June.

It turned out that Bill hadn't tied down the drill or the steel. Three passengers were sitting on top of the load, and when it shifted, there was no hope of bringing the airplane out of the spin.

Ron Wells took Bill's place flying for Transprovincial. During his years with the company he had three engine failures between Terrace and Telegraph Creek. In each case he was able to get the airplane down without too much damage and walk away from it.

One afternoon when I flew in to Lakelse Lake, Lloyd Johnson said he hadn't heard from Doug Chappell and asked me to go up and look for him. Doug had flown Bill Colburn and Ralph Menzies

Transprovincial Air Carriers' Otter at Arctic Lake in the Stikine River area.

up to Humphrey Creek that morning. Other planes joined the search later, but there was no sign of them. Lloyd called Air and Sea Rescue, which came the next day.

As it happened, the Rawleigh's salesman was driving along the road from Kitimat when he saw a man climb up the bank and onto the road. It was Doug. His ear and nose were nearly ripped off, his body badly banged up, and his clothes torn to pieces. The fellow drove him to Lakelse, and Lloyd took him to the hospital.

Doug said that he'd gone down at the head of Humphrey Creek, and the airplane was lying in water, snow, and boulders. Bill was dead and Ralph had a broken back. When a rescue team picked up Ralph, he said that Doug had leaned him against a huge windfall, told him he'd return, and jumped off the other side of the windfall. Ralph didn't know if he'd even survived the jump, and he sat there for two days wondering if help would ever come.

I was also involved in a search for one of Omineca Airways' Super Cubs in 1965. Omineca was owned by Bill Harrison from Tchesinkut Lake. Dick Schreiber, Omineca's pilot, had been flying ten-gallon drums of gas from Stewart up to a mining exploration

Pilots Ron Wells (right) and Pat Clay with Transprovincial Air Carriers' Otter at Glore Creek on the Stikine River. They were flying barrels of fuel into a mining operation.

camp. He'd been doing that all summer and was on his last trip. He had already sent his wife out to Prince Rupert on the *Camosun*. He headed up the Salmon Valley Pass. Somebody saw him climbing up into or behind a big cloud bank. They heard a winding up of the engine and he never came back.

Tony and I went with Doug Chappell in the Beaver as spotters. We stayed overnight in Stewart and ate breakfast before heading out. I was sitting in the back of the airplane, watching the rock wall on our left as we climbed. I looked out the right window and there was rock just off the right wing, too. I looked out the windshield and all I saw was rock!

Just then Doug kicked the left rudder and did a hammerhead. We went 2,000 feet down a creekbed, crossed the valley, and went up the rocks again. He repeated this several times. I almost lost my greasy breakfast. That was one of the roughest days of continuous flying I've ever had. The wind and turbulence and snow never let up, and we were flying tight against the mountainsides. As we crossed over from one side of the valley to the other, we hit a downdraft and went down 1,900 feet, hitting the bottom like we'd hit the rocks! The seat belts just about cut our legs off.

John Williams, owner of Wedeen River Logging Co., and Doug Chappell, chief pilot and shareholder of Transprovincial Air Carriers, at Terrace. The wheel-skis on the Otter allow it to land on bare ground or snow.

We gave up the search after a few days. Dick was found a week later. He had gone into a spin, came down with that gasoline behind him, and the airplane blew up.

We were using the Super Cub quite a lot in our business at that time. It hauled everything from tobacco to a cross-member for a D8 cat, which weighed 460 pounds. It took four of us to get it in, and we damned near wrecked the airplane doing it. We found that some things—like propane, acetylene, and oxygen—were very hard to load, so we decided to get a new airplane.

Our choice was between a Cessna 180 and a 185. We considered a Founds, which was a Canadian-built airplane. They made only fourteen of them. We looked at the Maule, a good little airplane, but with a step that we'd have to lift everything over. The Cessna could have planks up to the door rail, so we could slide the cargo into it. There was lots of room in the back and we would put plywood on the floor.

We traded in the Super Cub on a brand new Cessna 180. It came right from the factory in Wichita, with a seaplane kit built into it. It arrived in Vancouver in February 1966. We bought it from the Maschauds at Westcoast Air Services. They took it apart, painted it, installed the radio gear, and put the floats on.

Catermole-Trethewey bought the Super Cub later on and crashed it. It was completely demolished.

10

More Road Building (1964-1969)

Our company was growing during the 1960s, and there was lots of work. We were building the main logging road in the Nass, which is now part of the Stewart-Cassiar Highway. We had one of the first D9s in the country, three direct-drive Caterpillar D8s and 36As, a 46A and two 48A D7Es. In the winter we'd bring the equipment to our shop in Terrace for overhauling.

In the summer of 1964 we had a couple of D8s working for the Department of Indian Affairs at Aiyansh. We were building a new village site for the people there. Olav Satre was a civil engineer in charge of the project. He hired us to build the roads and streets. As we got to know him, he told of moving down from Alaska and buying a ranch in the Tatlayoko Valley in the Chilcotin. He often talked about his son Sven, who was finishing university in California that year. He asked if we might have a job for him later on, swamping on one of the cats.

Sven did come to work for us, and he was a very good cat swamper. He was especially interested in power-saw work and falling. We contracted out the job of falling right-of-ways to him for a dollar a tree. He partnered with a fellow from Fort St. John, George Aule. We got them a little eight-by-eight box of a trailer on a farm wagon. They lived in terrible conditions. When we'd pick them up at four in the morning to go to work, there'd be a big cloud of steam come out of the trailer from wet socks and boots and bone-dry pants. They worked hard and did a good job for us, and by that fall they were all monied up. George went back to Fort St. John and Sven went to Australia for a holiday. He said he'd be back the next year. It was 32 years before he returned.

During the time that we were building the road near New Aiyansh, Tony and I were home one weekend when Bill McCabe phoned up. He was the road-building superintendent for Columbia Cellulose.

"Can you boys go back early and start to plough that heavy snow off the Nass River Road and the logging roads?" he asked.

"Sure. We'll go out tomorrow," I said.

On Sunday, as we drove out, we found that there was already two and a half feet of snow, and it was still coming down. We had 60 miles to go to reach the area where we were going to plough. We had chains on the front wheels of the pickup, and a drum of gas and some shovels in the back. We couldn't go very fast because the snow was light, so whenever we speeded up it would fly over the hood and plug up the radiator.

Our plan was for Tony to run me down to the lower Nass, where I'd get my cat. Then I'd plough my way back along the river to my trailer, get some fuel and grub, then plough all night. Tony was going to head back north and open up that area. It was near dark as we approached the valley. Snow turned to rain and we were soon breaking trail through bumper-deep wet snow. As we continued on, the snow dropped but the rain poured down. The snowbanks were four feet high on both sides of the road.

We were going up a long hill when we saw in the headlight beam a huge wall of water and snow rushing toward us. We tried backing up, but it caught up with us. In the pitch-black night, with no backup lights, we ended up down in a swale in the road. We sat there for a minute, wondering what to do. The water and snow rose up quickly around us. Then the engine quit. We decided to abandon ship, but we couldn't push the doors open!

The snow was packed up against them. After getting the windows open, we managed to climb into the box. We quickly looked over the situation with our flashlights and decided we'd better get out of there, "toot- sweet." We took a big jump into the snowbank and went down to our necks in snow and water. Crawling and swimming through the slush, we managed to reach the road at the other side of the swale.

When we shone our flashlights back, all we could see was the top of the cab sticking out of the water. There we were, soaking wet and cold, with our flashlight batteries nearly dead. We walked five miles in a single track through the snow, back to our work trailer.

What a night! But that's how the northwest was opened up.

In 1966 Marj and I went to visit Sven in Australia. The next year I went back with the idea of going into business there. I'd been to the Caterpillar factory in Melbourne the year before, and they'd flown me all across the country. There were many opportunities to clear land and build beef roads. In Western Australia they were still driving the cattle out to Freemantle. It took months. Tony and I had talked about each of us spending six months there and six months in B.C. Equipment would be cheaper, and we wouldn't have to pay the horrendous taxes and duty. I sure thought hard about the great opportunity, but in the end we didn't take advantage of it.

Later in 1967, Tony and I were invited to visit the Caterpillar factory in Peoria, Illinois. We spent several days touring the plant, which was under 37 acres of roof. It was especially interesting to see the final assembly and testing of the machines. They were connected to a big cement post by a large chain attached to the drawbar, with the tracks sitting in two fifteen-foot slots for slippage. The machines were then run at different speeds, using each of the gears for certain lengths of time, which tested the power shift transmission and checked temperatures and pressures.

Fosbery Bros. Construction Ltd. bought the TH Ranch at Hanceville in the Chilcotin in 1967. Eve Fosbery ran the store and post office for many years.

That same year I heard that the old TH Ranch at Hanceville was for sale. I talked to the owner, Rene Hance, and Tony and I had a good long look at it. It was run down but had lots of potential, and our company had the equipment to put it into shape, so we decided to buy it.

Our mother was about to retire from Terrace Transfer, so we asked her if she'd like to run the store and post office at the ranch. She said, "Yes." She had always loved the Chilcotin. Incidentally, the post office had been on the ranch for 85 years.

We hired Lawrie Haines to run the ranch. We sold the cattle off to make it easier for him and our mother. We were so busy up north that we couldn't help them. Lawrie was a good cat operator, so we shipped a D7 down for him. He levelled a lot of land, cleared fence lines, and built an airstrip.

We tried to visit the ranch a few times a year. In the spring of 1969, Marj and I and our two youngest daughters, five-year-old Patti and three-year-old Margot, drove down to do some work on the place. Marj was going to paint some of the buildings

Tex and Marj Fosbery's daughters—Jan, Margot, Patti, and Joy—in 1968.

while I was seeding the fields. I was going to plant alfalfa, along with a cover crop of oats. I'd made arrangements to buy oat seed from Dan Lee and his sons Brud and Robin at Lee's Corner. When I drove the short distance over to get it, the girls came along for the ride. I was loading the oats into the pickup by hand with a big scoop shovel. Soon the girls asked if they could play in it.

"Sure you can," I said as I lifted them up into the box. When I finished loading, the girls were having such fun that I left them there for the ride home.

The ranch yard was on a sidehill, and before I'd gone for the oats I'd parked the tractor and seeder facing downhill toward the field. Now I pulled up the hill and backed gently down until the pickup touched the seeder.

The girls continued playing in the oats while I filled the seed boxes. When I was finally ready to go, I asked them, "Do you girls want to get out of there and go see your mum?"

"Not right now," they answered.

So I left them, got on the tractor, and drove down through the open gate. There was a curve in the road as it went onto the plank bridge across the irrigation ditch. As I swung to cross the bridge, I looked back at the girls. To my horror I saw the pickup starting to roll backwards down the hill. Patti was on the ground near the left rear wheel, pushing on the bumper to try to stop it. Margot was sitting in the middle of the load, facing me.

The truck picked up speed, heading for the gate. It was a straight line through the gate, across the field, through a barbed wire fence and some willow brush to the Chilcotin River.

I jumped off the tractor and ran toward the truck as it raced through the gate. I guess subconsciously I thought I could somehow stop it. Fortunately the truck missed the bridge and hit the irrigation ditch. The force of the sudden stop broke the tailgate latches, and Margot and the oats shot out from the box as if from a cannon. They landed in a pile in the field.

As I ran over I could hear her crying. She was practically buried. She had oats in her mouth and in her ears. I dug it away and checked her over. She didn't have a scratch on her!

Patti came running down the hill and the three of us sat there for a long time, holding onto each other. They didn't realize what might have happened, but I did and said a prayer of thanks. I almost lost my two dear little girls. I blamed myself for not blocking a wheel; it would have been a terrible price to pay.

By this time, back in Terrace, Columbia Cellulose had been sold and we were out of a job. We got on with EuroCan Pulp and Paper, a Finnish company that had just bought up a lot of timber around Ootsa Lake and planned on building a pulp mill in Kitimat. They were going to bring the timber up through Ootsa and Tahtsa Lakes and then haul it down to Kemano. There were about 35 miles of road to be built from the saltchuck up onto the plateau. It would be the fifth outlet to the Pacific in B.C.

One day I made a flight from Lakelse Lake to Kemano. I had the airplane loaded down with cutting edges and corner bits.

*Cat operator
Jack Butler (right)
and his swamper,
Ricky Scotton,
in the Nass Valley
in 1968.*

These are the extreme wear areas on bulldozer blades, and they made a very heavy load. I spent extra time tying them down to the floor. I also had a new dozer operator as a passenger.

It was late in the day and the weather was deteriorating, with the wind picking up. I was in a hurry. Flight service said the wind was gusting to 50 at the airport. I checked everything for takeoff. It looked good and off we went. I decided to shortcut through the mountains, though it was very turbulent. Ten minutes into the flight we hit a wind shear, turned upside down, and headed for the ground.

In my haste, I hadn't seen that my passenger had left his belt undone. He came right out of his seat. To this day I don't know how I got out of that situation. When the airplane came upright we were nearly in the rocks and trees, and heading in the opposite direction. I decided then that I should take an aerobatic course. The opportunity came in that winter of 1969, when I went to Florida. The ten-hour course increased my confidence considerably.

*One of the cats moving some "small stones" that
came down on the new road at Kemano.*

I took the long way home from Florida, visiting Lima in Peru
and Bogota, Colombia. I hired a guide, and we drove west into
the Honda Valley, which is ranching country. For a couple of
days I stayed on a ranch that had 4,000 head of cattle and a
contract with Russia to sell its beef for 70 cents a pound. There
was lots of grass and water and no hay to put up. All the work
was done with saddlehorses. A Russian Jeep was the only
mechanical equipment on the place. It seemed like Paradise,
but as always, there were some snakes in it. Banditos were a
problem. You had to sleep with one eye open.

Back on *our* ranch, things were going really well. Occasionally
I'd fly down to Fletcher Lake and my mother would drive me to
the ranch. That D7 was the only cat in the country for hire, so it
was going all the time. We had to buy a lowbed for it. Lawrie
didn't get to spend much time on the ranch, but he was making
money to help pay for it.

During these years our company had up to 28 people working
between Kemano, the Nass River, and the Chilcotin. We had two
D9s, five D8s, two D7s, as well as lowbeds and camps and all

*Hazel Henry, Eve Fosbery, and Veera Bonner with
the Fosbery Bros.' Cessna 180 at Fletcher Lake.*

that goes with this kind of work. In 1969 we were also building a logging campsite for EuroCan at Kildala Arm, an inlet that runs from Douglas Channel into the mountains. We took a cat, trailer, and a 2,000-gallon fuel tank over on a barge and unloaded it and the operator, Ivan Julsrud. I told him I'd fly in the next day. He was going to build a trail to better ground to set up the trailer.

I came back early the next morning. There was a low sea fog, and I couldn't see the water. I got down really low. I knew the fog wasn't very thick. I guessed that it was about half the height of the trees. I knew approximately where the cat was, so I got lined up and started to let myself down into the fog. I was making a long run. As I started settling down into the fog I checked that my airspeed and my descent were right. I let her go and go and then I was on the water. I couldn't see a thing. I shut the engine off and climbed out onto the float. I yelled into the fog, "Ivan!"

He answered and I fired up the airplane and headed toward his voice. I had to stop and listen once again before I made it. I shouldn't have done it, but I did, and I got away with it. I could have hit a log or I could have gone in at too steep an angle, dug the floats, and flipped her over on her back.

I helped Ivan get set up and then left him to build the campsite. Four days later I flew over, and I couldn't believe my eyes. He hadn't done a thing. He was standing on the shore as I pulled in. I said, "What's the matter?"

"Just a few hours after you left I broke all the spokes in the sprocket. I didn't have enough tools. I couldn't even jack it up." He was so frustrated. He'd had no way to get in touch with us. We both flew out.

We had an old six-wheeled army truck with a Hyab crane on it. I knew we could get close to the cat by going along Alcan's powerline road, which ran between Kemano and Kitimat. Our mechanic and Ivan went in, got the cat fixed, and Ivan got the job completed. I flew him out, but we couldn't get a barge to go in and get the equipment, so finally I rented a cedar raft from some loggers. It had a triple deck to give it flotation. I arranged for them to bring the raft in at high tide, tie it on the beach, and come back the next morning to tow it up the inlet to one of Alcan's base stations.

I had a kid helping me load the equipment. We were working at night, using the lights on the cat. I had to pull the trailer on and unhook it, then turn the cat and get the fuel tank. There were two-foot spaces between the logs of the raft, and when I was half turned, the cat slipped off the logs. It was sitting on its belly pan with the tracks hanging in the air. We gathered driftwood from the beach to put under the tracks. It was dark and muddy and it took us over two hours. By the time we finished we were played out. I said, "Let's go to bed."

We went into the trailer and lay down. As soon as we did, we heard the sound of scurrying feet. I shone my flashlight toward the sound. It was like looking down Granville Street: all those little eyes shining. The place was alive with mice!

When the tide came in, the boat came, towed us up the inlet, pushed us onto a nice ramp, unhooked, and tied the raft to shore. We went back to sleep. I woke up feeling as though I was standing up in my bed. The dishes started falling out of the cupboards, and the teapot fell off the stove. As the tide went out, the raft was tipping, and we were standing at a 35-degree angle! Eventually the tide came back in, and the raft became level again.

A barge came from Kitimat later on and picked up the equipment. I came down from Terrace and met it at EuroCan's dock. As it docked I jumped on the barge and started the cat. One of the fellows on the barge ran up to me and asked, "What the hell do you think you're doing?"

"I'm warming it up before it gets unloaded," I said.

"You don't touch anything on this barge," he said. "I belong to the longshoreman's union and it's up to us to do the work on the barge."

"It doesn't make sense to me," I replied. "It's my cat, but if you want to unload it, fly at it."

The lowbed that I'd hired came along and I walked the cat over to it and was about to put it onto the bed. The driver ran over, waving his arms. I thought he must not be ready for me to load, so I stopped. "What do you think you're doing?" he asked. "You can't load this cat. Are you a teamster?"

"No," I said. "I don't belong to any bloody union."

"Well I'm a teamster and this is part of my job," he said. "I'll put it on and I'll take it off."

"You don't make the payments on this thing so where are you coming from?" I said, while thinking to myself, "What in the name of God is this world coming to?"

11

Beginning of the End
(1969-1970)

Up to now we'd always managed to stay clear of the unions. We paid our good men better than union rate, and our everyday people got union rate. We had a different type of men, too. They were farm boys from the Cariboo, Peace River, and the prairies. They were glad to have a job and they did a good job for us. We treated them fairly and never had any problems.

In the fall of 1969, when we finished the road at Kemano, we shipped our equipment back to Terrace. Our company had been promised work, but when we arrived, there wasn't much available.

We did get a contract with Dawson Construction to build five miles of right-of-way along the Skeena River on the highway to Rupert. I took the first D8 down there and was unloading it off the lowbed beside the cold, windy river.

A big fancy car pulled up, and a guy in a suit and overcoat got out. He put on his rubbers and walked over to me. I got off the cat. "What's going on here?" he asked.

"Who wants to know?" I replied.

He said, "I represent local 115 union. This looks like the area where Dawson is building a new piece of road. Are you with Dawson?"

"No," I said. "I'm the contractor for the right-of-way."

"Are you certified with the 115?" he asked.

"No. We don't belong to any unions," I replied.

"Well, you won't be working here unless you get yourself certified," he said. "And I don't know whether we'll certify you or not."

That night we phoned the manager of Dawson Construction. He said, "God, aren't you fellows with the union?"

"No," I said.

"Well, you've already signed the contract. What are you going to do?" he asked.

We had thought about it and decided that we wanted to keep our boys working. I said, "I guess we'll have to bite the bullet and deal with the 115."

They got in touch with us in a couple of days. It was unbelievable what we had to go through. They had the authority to look at our financial statements. They questioned us about whether we were bona fide contractors, suitable to have their union people working for us. They said that a teamster would drive our crew to work in our crummy—and that's all he'd do! He'd sit in the vehicle all day and then drive the men home at quitting time. We were able to keep most of our boys. It had been suggested that they might have to go to the bottom of the list and be hired through the union hall in Prince George.

Later on we rented a Bucyrus Erie with a grapple, which we used to pile stumps and debris for burning. Since we didn't have an operator for it, we had to get one from the union hall. It was arranged for him to come out on the bus, stay at the Lakelse Hotel on Sunday night, and come down to the job on Monday morning. Travel and accommodation were at our expense. Two men came out and looked over the situation before one came that stayed. We had to drive the other two back to Terrace, where they stayed another night at the hotel before returning to Prince George. They didn't want to work. They just wanted to see the country and visit their friends. I've always said that unions and government made it very difficult to operate a business.

We got through the winter, finished the job, and went in the hole on it. We were so fed up, and now we were locked in with the 115. Tony and I figured that we couldn't have that hanging around our necks for years to come, so we decided that it was time for a change.

We called Stewart Equipment, who were auctioneers in Edmonton. We had bought a lot of equipment from them over the years and knew them pretty well. We asked if they would have a sale in Terrace, and they agreed to do one.

They brought out shop trucks, paint trucks, and mechanics and moved into our shop. Our equipment needed a few repairs and some painting. The sale date was to be June 21, 1970.

We were concerned about buyers, but they said, "If people will come to a sale in Edmonton, they'll come to one in Terrace."

They did come. At that time there were three jets a day flying into Terrace. Once it became known that we were having a sale, other contractors decided to get involved, and it turned into a good-sized sale.

Stewart Equipment sent out catalogues across the country. There were people attending the sale from as far away as New Brunswick. One of the cats went to Winnipeg, two to the Yukon, and the rest of the equipment stayed in B.C. We kept a D9, an 8240 Euclid, a Kenworth and lowbed, and the D7 cat at the ranch. That sale ended a very successful 23 years in B.C.'s northwest.

I had seen many changes throughout my working life, particularly in equipment and transportation. Cattle drives to a railway centre were a thing of the past, and stopping houses at frequent intervals along the roads were no longer necessary. In the logging industry, men with chainsaws had largely been replaced by machinery, and road-building equipment was bigger and more efficient. Many of the changes were for the better and many were not, but I'd enjoyed seeing them all.

Tony and I had been through some hard times during our partnership. Often there were just the two of us on a job somewhere out in the bush—building roads, logging, or mining. The business had depended on each of us doing the best we could in every situation. During the 1960s, a cat swamper who worked for us wrote the following poem. He only had a Grade 4 education.

There is a place where few people have ever been
Somewhere in the far northwest
That has an abundance of rock and mud
And millions of insect pests.

There's a road building job at this desolate place
Long hours, hard work and no sex.
The boys grumble an say What the hell do you expect?
When you are working for Tony and Tex.

In the fall theres the odd moose wandering round
To make hunters feel right at home
As long as he dont mind a little sleet and snow
And getting wet and chilled to the bone.

There is very nice scenery and plenty of lakes
It's really a beutifull place
But the cat skinners rave as they sink in the mud
Or creep a long a sheer rock face.

The mornings are chilly but cheerful
There is never a sign of gloom
The boys happily put on their mackinaws
And go outside to the dining room.

If you want to work for Tony and Tex
Out among the evergreen trees
Just grab your packsack and gumboots
And head for the Quinageese.

Epilogue

It was time to take on a new challenge. Tony and Betty moved to their property west of Alexis Creek and began developing a ranch. Marj and I had separated, so she and the girls remained in Terrace, and I moved to the TH Ranch. It was good to be back in the Cariboo.

The ranch was located at a beautiful spot on the Chilcotin River. It included a thousand acres of deeded land and a thousand-acre lease. The Hances had been very successful on the ranch for two generations. Tom Hance had come there in 1898 and started the place as a trading post. He was a packer as well, and wintered his packhorses there. His sons—Rene, Grover, and Percy—later developed it into a cattle and guest ranch. When I bought it, they were getting on in years and still doing things the old way.

We were living in a different era, and my company had access to newer equipment. There was a big spring behind the barn, which produced 1,165 gallons of water a minute. A gravity system brought the water to the buildings. Eventually we put in an irrigation system using electric pumps so that more land could be put into hay production. The temperature of the water stayed at 52 degrees, so the cattle didn't have to drink ice-cold water in the winter.

I made arrangements with Alex and Ann Paxton to bring their cattle to the ranch on a share basis. We built the herd up to 200 head over the years and kept them all on ranch property. I made every piece of the property productive, with good hay crops

The TH Ranch buildings at Hanceville in 1973. The ranch was located on the Chilcotin River and ran 200 head of cattle. Notice the barn at the ranch with the brand painted on the roof. It had six stalls and a tack room.

and pastures. We also had quite a collection of farmyard pets, of which Arnold, the pig, was one of my favourites. He followed me everywhere, including underneath vehicles when I was working on them. He'd crawl in and lie up against my back, grunting contentedly. My mother didn't like his habit of eating anything in sight: nuts and bolts, a bag of mortar, chocolate bars. He even ate two boxes of Tide and then blew bubbles from both ends!

Charlie Brown was an orphan calf that we kept for six years. He was the best cowboy on the ranch, leading the cattle eighteen miles to their grazing area each spring and bringing them back in the fall.

During the years at the ranch, Tony and I started a new road construction company. We brought down a few machines that we still had up north and formed Battle Mountain Construction. We had one of our old employees, Ed Davis, take charge of it. We all kept busy until 1972, an election year in B.C., when we got a new NDP government. There wasn't much work for the construction company, and the economy didn't look very good,

Tex's house at the TH Ranch. A spring behind the barn
provided water for the irrigation system seen on the hay fields.

so we sold most of the equipment. Tony and I decided to sell the ranch, too, and after twenty years we dissolved our partnership.

The ranch was bought and sold once or twice after I left, and eventually it went into receivership. The bank sold it off in small parcels, so it's not a working ranch anymore.

Tony and his second wife, Sheila, moved to a small farm near Sorrento, where they still live.

I moved to a small acreage with a house on it at Lac la Hache. I still had two cats, which Don Durrell and I were running. In 1975 we were down at Spuzzum, building logging roads for Catermole-Trethewey. When I wasn't working away, I was building up the place at Lac la Hache.

I was also doing a lot of flying. In 1977 I flew across Canada with Ron Wells in my Cessna 180. Mel Stewart and his son David went along with us in their 172. Ron had flown for Transprovincial Air Carriers for many years and was one of the best flyers to ever sit in an airplane. We flew from Williams Lake to Inuvik, where we stayed for several days. We then carried on to Waterville, Nova Scotia, camping out along the way. The weather in the east was terrible. In one place I was following some railway

"The boss"! Arnold at the TH Ranch, probably looking for something to get into. He once ate two boxes of Tide and blew bubbles from both ends.

tracks, and the fog forced me down so low that I nearly hit a train. In Waterville we visited Leslie Hutchison, who had worked for us at Kitimat. The round trip was 9,000 miles, and took 64 hours of flight time.

In 1979 I started discing and seeding rangeland throughout B.C. for the Ministry of Agriculture. For six years I worked at that job and met a lot of interesting people.

Dad died of pneumonia in 1984, at the age of 86. He spent his last years living in East Kelowna and is buried in the Lumby cemetery.

Mother died at Williams Lake in 1985, at the age of 81. I scattered her ashes from the airplane over the Home Place, the Bar 5 Ranch at Big Creek.

In 1985 I spent five months working for Northway Mining at Henderson Creek, in the Yukon, and the next year I started working in the Cariboo, building logging roads. I have continued doing that kind of work, although I've also had time to enjoy life.

In 1992, my friend Edith MacKay, my granddaughter Sarah, and I made a trip down the Mackenzie River in my jet boat. We started at Hay River and travelled 1,032 miles to Inuvik. The trip took ten days, including a stop of four days in Norman Wells due to bad weather. The actual travelling time was 40 hours and 30 minutes.

In March 1993 I drove from Williams Lake to Inuvik, picked up Joy's daughter Meghan, and drove over the sea ice to Tuktoyaktuk. The ice road, which was maintained by the government of the Northwest Territories, was twelve feet thick.

In 1994 Sven and Denise Satre returned to the Chilcotin with their two sons and bought a ranch at Tatlayoko. Sven had worked for 32 years in the South Pacific area, where I had visited him several times. His move back to Canada was to end in tragedy. One day Sven and his hired man were returning from checking the cows on the range. They each took a different route, and when Sven didn't arrive, Denise and a small search party tried to find him, but it became too dark.

At daylight, they hiked up the trail and found Sven's horse, with the halter shank still attached to the saddle, which was on the ground. Farther along they saw a black bear, and as they approached it, they saw Sven lying dead on the ground.

Denise and the boys moved back to Australia, and in August 1998 they returned to Canada to sell the ranch. They, along with friends and family, placed a brass plaque at the spot where Sven lost his life.

My daughters Jan and Margot live in Victoria, Patti lives in Terrace, where she has spent most of her life, and Joy lives in Inuvik, where she's been for several years. Marj is remarried and lives in Terrace. Lynn and I have lived in Williams Lake for the past several years.

In 2000 I continue to do some road building, fly my airplane, and visit old friends. I have also made several trips down the Yukon River. As well as travelling in this great country of ours, I enjoy reading the history of it. I guess now that Karen has heard all this, she plans to make me part of it.

Notes

1 The Becher House was a stopping house on the Chilcotin Road. It was built by Fred Becher in 1915. In the early 1940s it was owned by Geneva Martin.

2 The Harper Ranch was part of the old Gang Ranch, established by brothers Thaddeus and Jerome Harper of Virginia in the 1860s. It is located on the South Thompson River near Kamloops. Sam Brookes bought it in the early 1940s and sold it a short time later to Irwin and Vi Kerr. They, and later their son Raymond, operated the ranch until 1999, when it was sold to the Kamloops Indian Band.

Index

Alaska Highway 121, 122
Alcan 124, 174
Alder Creek (BC) 152-155
Alexandra Lodge 104, 109
Alexis Creek (BC) 11, 48, 52, 181
Anahim Lake (BC) 47, 49-50
Anahim Reserve 47, 51
Anahim Stampede 49-50
Arctic Lake (BC) 162
Arlington Roadhouse 83
Arnold 182, 184
Ashcroft (BC) 10, 11, 19, 47
Aule, George 165

B.C. Equipment 136
Bald Mountain (BC) 36, 38
Ballarat Creek (YT) 137
Bambrick, Charlie 15
Bank of Nova Scotia 127
Bar 5 Ranch 184
Baronoff Hotel 63
Battle Mountain Construction 182
Bear Creek (BC) 20-24
Bear Creek School 21
Beaumont Ranch 35
Becher House 28, 30, 32-33, 35, 36, 44
Bedrock Creek (YT) 78
Bell Ranch 11
Big Creek (BC) 9-13, 15-18, 21, 184
Big Creek School 18
Blenkinsop, Fay 18
Blenkinsop, Gerald 19, 24-25
Blenkinsop, Neville 18
Blenkinsop, Queenie 24-25
Bliss, Jack 48, 51
Bliss, June 48, 51
Bonanza Creek (YT) 70
Bonner, Veera Witte 18, 173
Boston Bar (BC) 110
Boundary (AK) 121
Boyde, Stanley 38, 39, 41-42
Bridge River (BC) 99, 101

Brookes, Sam 34
Bushell, Bill 85
Butler, Jack 171

Cache Creek (BC) 104
California Creek (YT) 86
Calumet Mine 77
Camosun 143
Campbell and Bennett 124, 134
Campbell, Bob 26
Canadian National Railway 55
Canadian Pacific Airlines 82
Canadian Pacific Railways 143
Canol Pipeline 121
Cariboo Gold Quartz 90
Carson, Mrs. 26
Carter, Nick 47
Casca 67-70
Cassiar Creek (YT) 72, 73
Cassidy (BC) 155
Catermole-Trethewey 164, 183
Caterpillar factory 167
Chappell, Doug 159, 161-164
Charlie Brown 182
Charters, Dr. 11
Cherry Creek Ranch 54
Chilanko Forks (BC) 48
Chilcotin River (BC) 93-94, 181
Chilko Ranch Store 14
Chilko River (BC) 51
Chilkoot Trail 9
China Bar (BC) 106
China Cabin (BC) 110
Church, Dick 10
Church, Percy 10
Clay, Pat 163
Colburn, Bill 161-162
Colley, Harry 77
Colombia 172
Columbia Cellulose Pulp and Paper 113, 114, 117, 123, 135-136, 166, 170
Columbia Construction 115-116, 140-141

Connon, Gus 52-55
Copper River (BC) 114, 147
Cotton, Mr. 28
Cotton Ranch 28, 47
Crowe, Howard 24

Daine, Charlie 21
Daine, Mrs. 21
Davis, Ed 182
Dawson City (YT) 65, 69, 70-71, 82-89, 117, 121
Dawson Construction 176-177
Dawson Creek (BC) 122
Dead Horse Gulch (AK) 64-65
Decker Lake (BC) 113
Department of Indian Affairs 165
Diamond Match Co. 156
Dole, Mr. 23, 62
Dougherty Place 82
Douglas Channel (BC) 173
Dowling, Stan 49, 50
Dunlop, Eva 93, 96
Dunlop, Hughie 93-97
Durrell, Don 183
Durrell, Harry 29-30, 38, 43, 45, 46
Durrell, Jack 29, 38-42, 43, 46
Durrell, Mrs. 43
Dychikowski, Bill 161
Dychikowski, Peter 156-158, 159, 161

Elkins, Joe 50
Elkins, Thomas 50-51
Elliot, Wes 89
EuroCan Pulp and Paper 170, 173
Evans, Art 103
Evans, Lloyd 136

F and F Café 85
Farwell Canyon (BC) 36, 93-95, 97-98, 99
Finning Tractor 127, 129, 137, 138, 141

Fleming, Bill 25
Fletcher Lake (BC) 173
Florida 172
Ford's Cove (BC) 128, 131-134
Fort Selkirk (YT) 68
Forty Mile River (YT) 62
Fosbery, Betty 103, 121, 137, 140, 141, 181
Fosbery Bros. Construction Ltd. 133, 155, 156, 165, 173: beginnings 128; airplanes 150, 152, 156, 158, 164, 173; and Australia 167; and TH Ranch 168, 182-183; and unions 175-178; closing-out sale 178-179
Fosbery, Eve Mary Napier 11-13, 15-18, 23, 24, 28, 34, 102, 168, 182, 184: photos 14, 17, 24, 146, 173
Fosbery, Helen 139-140
Fosbery, Jan 141, 146, 169, 185
Fosbery, Joy 151, 169, 185
Fosbery, Margot 168-170, 185
Fosbery, Marj Kennedy 102-104, 106, 107, 109, 110, 112, 114, 118, 121, 130, 132-133, 141, 167, 168, 181, 185: photos 103, 122, 146
Fosbery, Patti 168-170, 185
Fosbery, Percy Henry Vincent "Bob" 9-13, 15-27, 34, 62-63, 65-66, 71, 73-74, 77-79, 81-82, 102, 127, 139-140, 184: photos 14, 16, 64, 72, 103, 146, 152
Fosbery, Percy Vincent (grandfather) 9, 10
Fosbery, Sheila 183
Fosbery, Texas: birth of 11; and school 18, 21-22, 26; quits school 28; first job 24-25; freezes ears 43-44; first car 51-55, 57; goes to Yukon 62-63; works in Wells mine 90-92; takes job with Int'l Pacific Salmon Commission 93; marries Marj Kennedy 103; moves to Terrace 114; returns to Yukon 117; returns to Terrace 123; goes into cat business 126; starts Fosbery Brothers with Tony 127; summer in Queen Charlottes 141-144; learns to fly 148-149; overseas trips 167, 172; wraps up company 178-179;

separates from Marj 181; moves to TH Ranch 181; starts new company 182; dissolves partnership with Tony 183; cross-Canada trip 183-184; photos 12, 16, 17, 23, 24, 26, 57, 58, 59, 63, 66, 72, 76, 82, 89, 97, 103, 110, 119, 126, 146, 150, 156, 159
Fosbery, Tony 22, 62, 73, 103, 122, 139-140, 143, 147, 157, 159, 163, 167, 181, 183: birth of 11; quits school 28; in Yukon 117, 119; goes to Yukon 63-68, 73-74, 78, 79-82, 84-85, 87, 90, 117, 119, 137; moves to Terrace 121; goes into business with Tex 128; in Portland Canal 128, 130; good mechanic 134, 136; working with Tex 132-136, 138-143, 145, 147, 155, 165-168, 178-179, 182-183; gets pilot's licence 156: photos 13, 16, 17, 24, 63, 72, 75, 82, 87, 103, 119
Foster, Jack 124-125
Four Mile Creek (BC) 32, 44
Fournier, Joe 88
Fraser Canyon (BC) 104
Fraser River (BC) 32

Gang Ranch 19, 36, 38
Gardener's mill 101, 102
Garland, Ed 31
Glore Creek (BC) 163

Haines, Lawrie 168, 172
Haller, Clarence 46-47
Haller, Lester 34, 35
Hance, Charlie 36-38
Hance, Grover 181
Hance, Percy 47, 181
Hance, Rene 47, 168, 181
Hance, Tom 181
Hanceville (BC) 41, 47, 51, 168, 182
Harper Ranch 34-35, 46, 55, 56-61
Harrison, Bill 162
Harrison, Helen 149
Hay River (NWT) 184
Hazelton (BC) 113
Hell's Gate (BC) 99, 103, 105-111, 114
Hembrough, Doug 96
Henderson Creek (YT) 184
Henry, Hazel 173
Hillcrest Ranch 30-32

Hodgson, Tommy 28, 43
Holbrook Camp 73-74, 77, 79, 81
Hootalinqua (YT) 67
Horsefly (BC) 24, 25-27, 82, 99, 101, 104, 110
Horsefly Lake (BC) 98, 101, 102
Horsefly Landing (BC) 102
Horsefly Road 110
Horseshoe Lake (BC) 38, 39, 42
Hotel Vancouver 46
Hubbard, Mrs. 99
Hume and Rumble Pole Company 102
Humphrey Creek (BC) 138, 162
Hunker Creek (YT) 66, 71
Hunker Dome Camp 88
Hutchinson, Bob 35-38
Hutchison, Leslie 184

Inlander Hotel 156
International Pacific Salmon Commission 93, 95, 98, 101, 112
International Woodworkers of America 117, 147
Inuvik (NWT) 183, 184, 185

Jack 99-100, 105, 108, 120, 122-123, 143
Jack-o'-Clubs Lake (BC) 90
Jasper, Delmer 33, 35, 47-50, 52, 98, 99
Jasper, Mabel 33, 52
Jasper, Wes 33, 49-50, 52
Jello Jack 74
Johnson, Bruce 124, 140
Johnson, Lloyd 157, 159, 161-162
Johnson, Willie 47, 48, 50
Julsrud, Ivan 173-174
Juneau (AK) 63

Kalamalka Lake (BC) 22
Kalum River (BC) 136
Kalum Valley (BC) 114
Kamloops (BC) 34, 55, 63
Kelly Lake (BC) 99
Kelowna (BC) 22, 27, 52
Kemano (BC) 170, 172-174, 176
Kennedy, Allen 112, 113, 132, 152-155
Kennedy, Mrs. 103, 110
Kennedy, Murray 106
Keno 68-69
Keno City (YT) 77
Kerr, Irwin 61-62
Kiested, Nels 83
Kildala Arm (BC) 173

Kitimat (BC) 123, 138-139, 141, 170, 174
Kitimat River (BC) 138, 139, 140
Klondike River (YT) 9, 83

Lac la Hache (BC) 27, 183
Laceese 13
Lake Bennett (BC) 65
Lake Laberge (YT) 65, 67
Lakelse (BC) 124
Lakelse Construction 138
Lakelse Hotel 177
Lakelse Lake (BC) 140, 156-159, 161, 170
Lakeview Hotel 25, 28, 33, 93
Lee, Brud 169
Lee, Dan 169
Lee, Ed 48
Lee, Robin 169
Lee's Corner (BC) 169
Legate Creek (BC) 116
Leland Hotel 55
Lewis River (YT) 67
Lillooet (BC) 99-101
Lincoln, Phyllis 26
Lindquist, Kenny 56, 90
Little, Dud 150
Little Horsefly River (BC) 99, 101-102
Little, Houghlund, and Kerr 113
Litzenberger's Livery Barn 36
London, Jack 70
Lowe, Mickey 34-35
Lumby (BC) 102, 139
Lytton (BC) 104

MacDonald, Mr. 129
MacDonald, Neil 123, 127, 133-134
MacKay, Donald 32
MacKay, Edith 184
MacKay, Isabella 32
Mackenzie River (NWT) 184
Mah, Cedric 159-160
Martin, Geneva 33, 35
Martin, Mickey 33, 35
Masset (BC) 141
Mayo (YT) 68-69
McCabe, Bill 166
McCormick's Transportation 83, 86
McKay, Emogene 29, 33
McKay, Hazel 29, 33
McKay, Joan 29, 33
McKay, "Little Mac" 29, 32, 33
McKay, Richard 29, 33
McLaughlin, Joe 31
McNaughton, George 98, 99
Medby, Ole 79-80, 88
Meldrum Creek (BC) 29
Menzies, Ralph 161-162

Meziadin Lake (BC) 159-160
Milk Ranch 47
Miller Creek (YT) 78, 79
Ministry of Agriculture 184
Minto (YT) 67
Moon, Charlie 28
Moon, Pudge 30-31
Mud River (BC) 112-113
Murphy Lake (BC) 35

Napier, Egbert 11
Napier, Esme 11
Nass River (BC) 138, 147, 150, 155, 165
Nass River Road 166
Nass Valley (BC) 171
Nelsen, Ragnar 82
Nelson Brothers' Fisheries 131
New Aiyansh (BC) 165-166
New Westminster Hotel 86
Newton, Mrs. 48, 51-52
Niquidet, George 104, 110
Norman Wells (NWT) 121, 185
North Bend (BC) 107
Northway Mining 184

Occidental Hotel 86
Okanagan 20
Okanagan Lake (BC) 20, 62
Okanagan Landing (BC) 20
Okanagan Mission (BC) 26, 27
Old Hazelton (BC) 156
Omineca Airways 162
150 Mile House (BC) 26, 35, 53, 54
Ootsa Lake (BC) 170

Pacific Great Eastern Railway 101
Palmantier, Leonard 47
Parker, Harry 24
Pavilion Mountain (BC) 99
Paxton, Alex 181
Paxton, Ann 181
Pearl Harbour Hotel 82, 84-85, 87
Pentona 62
Peoria (IL) 138, 167
Perry, Brownie 32
Perry, Stanley 29
Peru 172
Piffko, Karen 185
Port Clements (BC) 141-142
Portland Canal (AK) 127, 131-133
Postak and MacDonald 123, 126, 130-134
Pothole Ranch 36-38
Powell River Pulp and Paper Company 34
Powers Creek (BC) 27
Prince George (BC) 112, 177

Prince Rupert (BC) 112, 114, 117, 123, 127, 130, 176
Princess Louise 63

Queen Charlotte Airlines 132, 133, 141
Queen Charlotte City (BC) 143
Queen Charlotte Islands (BC) 141
Quilt, Louis 19

Rafferty's Store 52
Raven Lake (BC) 38-39, 42-46
Rayleigh (BC) 34
Red Jacket Lodge 99
Redstone (BC) 48
Regina Hotel 71
Remo (BC) 135
Rennie, Bob 105
Riske Creek (BC) 28, 29, 36, 37, 50, 52, 95, 96
RivTow Tug and Barge 147
Roberts, Bert 93, 96
Roberts, Bob 93
Rose Spit (BC) 142

Salmon Valley Pass (BC) 163
Salvas (BC) 147
Sandspit (BC) 141
Sansouci 87
Sargent, Bill 156
Satre, Denise 185
Satre, Olav 165
Satre, Sven 165-166, 167, 185
Savona (BC) 54
Sawmill Creek (BC) 24, 42
Schmidt, Harold 117, 119, 137
Schreiber, Dick 162, 164
Scotton, Ricky 171
Seal Cove (BC) 130
Semsmo, Ovi 79-81
Seymour, Danny 59
Shames (BC) 117, 129, 135, 137
Sheep Creek (BC) 30
Sheep Creek Bridge 32
Sixty Mile (YT) 71, 73-79, 80, 81, 117-121
Sixty Mile River (YT) 76
Skagway (AK) 63-64
Skeena River (BC) 113, 117, 123, 126, 145, 150-152, 176
Skoglund Logging 123, 147, 150
Skoglund, Ray 138
Slee Place 29, 38, 41, 42
Sogoff, Harry 74
Sorrento (BC) 183
Spences Bridge (BC) 104
Spuzzum (BC) 183
Squamish (BC) 46

St. Mary's Hospital (Dawson City) 83
Steamboat Mountain 122
Steinhelber, Les 67, 71
Stewart (BC) 133, 162-163
Stewart, David 183
Stewart Equipment 178-179
Stewart, Mel 183
Stewart River (YT) 68-69
Stewart-Cassiar Highway 161, 165
Stikine River (BC) 162, 163
Stone, Charlie 74
Stuart, Harold 52
Stutts, Hans 55
Sugarcane Reserve 53
Sullivan Bay (BC) 149

Tahtsa Lake (BC) 170
Tatlayoko (BC) 185
Tatlayoko Valley (BC) 165
Tchesinkut Lake (BC) 162
Terrace (BC) 113-117, 121, 123, 126, 127, 134-136, 138, 139, 144, 148, 150, 164, 170, 176, 178
Terrace Hotel 135
Terrace Transfer 168
Teslin River (YT) 67
TH Ranch 168, 172- 173, 179, 181-184
The Tunnels (BC) 106

Thirty Mile River (YT) 67
Thompson, Mr. 106, 107, 109
Thompson River (BC) 19
Tok Junction (AK) 71, 86
Toosey Reserve 37
Top of the World Highway 71, 82
Towdystan (BC) 48
Transprovincial Air Carriers 156, 157, 159-164, 183
Trapper Lake (BC) 161
Tuktoyaktuk (NWT) 185

Vancouver (BC) 46, 63, 103
Vancouver Aero Club 148-149
Vanderhoof (BC) 112-113
Vavenby (BC) 55-56
Vedan, Louis 17

Walsh, Joe 74
Walters, Gilbert 26
Walters, Leonard 26
Waterville (NS) 183
Watson Island (BC) 117
Webster, Jardie 26
Webster, Marilyn 26
Webster, Maxine 26
Webster, Murray 118
Webster, Ray 26, 112, 113, 116, 118
Wedeen River Logging Co. 164
Wells (BC) 90

Wells, Ron 161, 163, 183
Westbank (BC) 23, 24, 27
Westcoast Air Services 164
Western Plywood 145
White Pass & Yukon Railway 64-65
Whitehorse (YT) 65-66, 121
Whitehorse Inn 65
Williams, John 164
Williams Lake (BC) 11, 15, 24, 25, 28, 32, 33, 36, 46, 47, 52, 93, 112, 183, 185
Williams Lake Motors 103
Witte, Duane 18
Witte, Hazel 18
Woodland, Tony 46
World War I 10
World War II 27
Wotzke, Herb 35, 56-57, 60
Wotzke, Randie 35, 56
Wotzke, Sam 56
Wright, Lynn 185
Wycotte, Fred 38-40, 43, 44

Yukon Consolidated Mining Company 88, 90
Yukon River (YT) 67, 69, 73, 79, 81, 185

Zirnhelt, Mr. 35

Texas Fosbery

Texas Fosbery, born in Big Creek in the Chilcotin area of B.C., has worn many hats in his life. He has been a nomad, hobo, cowboy, labourer, miner, cat-skinner, logger, road-builder, pilot, rancher, adventurer, father, and friend.

He has spent 73 years in many parts of this country, particularly in B.C. and the Yukon. From his beginnings at Big Creek he moved to the Okanagan, then back to the Chilcotin, Kamloops, Dawson City, Horsefly, Lillooet, Hell's Gate, Terrace, Kitimat-Kemano, Queen Charlotte Islands, Hanceville, Lac la Hache, and Williams Lake.

Tex loves life and has made the most of it.

About the Author

Karen Piffko was born in Kamloops in 1942. Her parents, Herb and Randie Wotzke, worked at the Harper Ranch, and it was there that she and Tex met in 1945. They didn't meet again until 1996, after nearly a lifetime had passed. Their chance meeting in Williams Lake led to the writing of Tex's biography.

Karen grew up and went to school in Williams Lake. After graduation she worked at the Bank of Commerce for two years before moving to Kenora and later Toronto. She returned to B.C. in 1972, living in Kelowna and Williams Lake, where she was employed by the Bank of Montreal.

In 1976 Karen and her husband, George Piffko, bought a hay farm at Big Lake. As well as working on the farm, Karen served on the board of the Big Lake Community Association for several years. After twenty years of farming, they retired, with George moving to Hagensborg and Karen remaining at Big Lake.

Karen has done freelance writing and photography for the *Williams Lake Tribune* for the past fifteen years. Her hobbies include travelling, kayaking, hiking, and cross-country skiing.